# North African
## Cooking

# North African
## Cooking

Tess Mallos

PERIPLUS

First published in the United States in 2006 by Periplus Editions (HK) Ltd.,
with editorial offices at 364 Innovation Drive, North Clarendon, VT 05759 and
130 Joo Seng Road, #06-01/03 Singapore 368357

Text, photography and design © 2005 Lansdowne Publishing Pty. Ltd.

ISBN-13 978-0-7946-5022-3
ISBN-10 0-7946-5022-8
Printed in Singapore

DISTRIBUTED BY

North America and Latin America (English Language)
**Tuttle Publishing**
364 Innovation Drive, North Clarendon, VT 05759-9436
Tel: (802) 773-8930  Fax: (802) 773-6993
Email: info@tuttlepublishing.com
www.tuttlepublishing.com

Japan
**Tuttle Publishing**
Yaekari Building 3F, 5-4-12 Osaki,
Shinagawa-ku, Tokyo 141-0032
Tel: (03) 5437-0171  Fax: (03) 5437-0755
Email: tuttle-sales@gol.com

Asia Pacific
**Berkeley Books (Pte) Ltd**
130 Joo Seng Road #06-01/03 Singapore 368357
Tel: (65) 6280-1330  Fax: (65) 6280-6290
Email: inquiries@periplus.com.sg
www.periplus.com

Commissioned by Deborah Nixon
Text: Tess Mallos
Photographer: Rob Reichenfeld
Stylist: Vicki Liley
Food Assistant: Georgina Leonard
Designer: Avril Makula
Cover Design: Bettina Hodgson
Editor: Susin Chow
Project Coordinator: Bettina Hodgson
Production: Sally Stokes and Eleanor Cant

Photographer and stylist for cover and pages 26, 27, 52, 89, 110, 115, 117, 119: Vicki Liley
Photographer page 30: Ben Dearnley
Photographer page 88: Louise Lister, Stylist: Suzie Smith
Photographer page 112: Alan Benson, Stylist: Marie-Helene Clauzon

Set in Univers 55 on QuarkXPress

# contents

# introduction

The cooking of North Africa and the spread of Islam are closely linked. After the death of the Prophet Mohammed in 632 CE, his followers wrote down his teachings creating the Koran. They began their task to spread the Prophet's message. In their push to the West, they had conquered Egypt in 641 CE, finishing in present-day Morocco in 683 CE. Gradually, North Africa gained a new religion, a new language, and new foods and recipes for the table.

North Africa is a land of contrasts. The Sahara, the largest desert in the world, spreads from Morocco to Tunisia, and joins the Libyan and Arabian deserts. It is dotted with life-giving oases, some just a pool surrounded by date palms, others with a township surrounding them; arable land and pasture hug the coast; and the Atlas mountains to the west cross Morocco and Algeria.

To the east is the oldest civilization, Egypt, dating back to 3200 BCE, with farming settlements along the Nile some 1300 years before that. Berber tribes inhabited the remainder of North Africa from 2400 BCE, either in settlements or nomadic, such as the Tuaregs who still roam the sandy wastelands today. The Berbers are a Caucasian people, believed to have originated in present-day Libya, and at the time of the Arab conquest, lived in Mauretania and Numidia (northern parts of today's Morocco and Algeria). Except for Egypt and Libya, the majority of North Africans are Berber but are described as Arab/Berber.

Many of the Berber customs continue to the present day, such as their moussems—festivals and pilgrimages. Vast tent cities are erected for the particular occasion. Both Morocco and Algeria are renowned for their moussems, where the delicious mechoui is prepared—whole lamb rubbed with a spice, garlic and ghee mixture, spit-roasted slowly and almost continually basted, until the meat can be torn off with the fingers in meltingly tender strips.

In 711 CE, Arabs, together with Berbers of Mauretania, invaded Spain. Collectively they were known as the Moors, after the Mauris of Mauretania. They named it Al Andaluz, and via Arabia and Persia they introduced the cultivation of the saffron crocus, various citrus fruits, rice and sugar cane, and the use of almonds and exotic spices in cooking. The Berber dynasties of the Almoravides and the Almohades, who ruled in Moorish Spain and north-west Africa between 1064 and 1269, with other Berber dynasties following, had lavish palace kitchens. The cooks were women, and through this means, new foods and recipes filtered into the communities.

The French colonized Algeria in 1830, and made Tunisia a protectorate in 1881 and Morocco in 1912. Besides defining borders, improving infrastructure and agriculture, planting vineyards and introducing viticulture, they introduced the second language still used in those countries. By 1962, the French had left the region, but their presence is still evident in some aspects of city life such as the café and epicerie. As far as food is concerned, their only legacy has been baguettes, croissants and a few patisserie items.

There is an admirably strong sense of family; all are present for the midday meal. The ritual hand-washing varies, but for a formal gathering, a family member circulates with a kettle of warm, rose-scented water, a basin and towel so that each diner can rinse the fingers of their right hand.

Dishes are served on a central platter, tagine or small bowls placed in the middle of a round table, with the diners seated on low divans or cushions. After the blessing, "Bismillah" (in the name of Allah), food is delicately picked from the section of the platter closest to the diner, using the thumb and first two fingers of the right hand and popped into the mouth. If necessary, fingers are wiped on the diner's piece of bread, never licked. Hands are washed more thoroughly at the end of the meal.

Ramadan is the ninth month of the Muslim year, commemorating Mohammed's first revelations that are the Koran. Muslims fast during Ramadan from dawn to dusk for 30 days—this means no food or drink as well as other restrictions. In the cities a canon is fired at the appropriate time and the first meal begins. Each country has its own traditions in breaking the fast —some eat dates and drink milk, others begin with a soup packed with protein foods and carbohydrates with bread, and sweet fried doughs follow. Another meal is served later in the evening, and before daybreak leftovers, dates, hard-cooked eggs, milk and sweet fried doughs or pastries fuel the body for the day's fast.

## MOROCCO

The cooking of Morocco showcases its history, and the wealth of ingredients now available to the cook—as it is a country blessed with rich, arable land, ample pastures and varying climate zones to produce foods in abundance. Moroccan cooking developed in the lavish court kitchens of the Berber dynasties of the Almoravides and the Almohades, who ruled in Al Andaluz and Morocco, in the cities of Fez, Meknes, Rabat and Marrakesh. Later Berber dynasties continued the process.

Its cuisine clearly shows Arab/Persian and Andalusian influences. The use of fruit in tagines is a perfect example of the Persian influences in Arabic cooking, such as Beef with Prunes and Almonds and Chicken with Apricots and Honey. Bistella, the famous pigeon or chicken pie of Morocco, is based on a Berber dish called trid; the filling is Berber, the almonds, sugar and cinnamon are Andalusian, and the pastry is Persian, which was based in turn on the spring roll wrappers of China.

The tissue-thin pastry used for bistella, and other sweet and savory pastries, is called warkha, Arabic for "leaf." It is not a rolled pastry like filo, but achieved in a process that requires skill and patience. A round, tin and copper pan, called a "tobsil," is heated over a gas flame or a pan of boiling water. The tobsil is greased lightly with an oily cloth and a ball of dough is expertly and rapidly tapped over the hot surface until the film of dough left behind with each tap becomes a complete sheet. When the surface is dry, the sheet is loosened and lifted off and the process begins again, and again

and again… It takes a few seconds but great skill to make each sheet. Each city and town has its warkha makers, and the Moroccan housewife prefers to leave it to the experts. Filo pastry is recommended for dishes that are baked, while spring roll wrappers can be used for fried pastries, as warkha has to be fried, not baked.

Tagines are the cornerstone of the Moroccan kitchen. The name for this stew comes from the Berber cooking pot—a shallow earthenware dish topped with a conical lid. However, tagines are mostly prepared in a saucepan on a modern stove, or even in a pressure cooker, then transferred to a tagine for serving. The tagine is made of lamb, beef, chicken or fish, flavored with aromatic onions and garlic, herbs and spices, and can include vegetables, fruits or olives, such as Chicken with Preserved Lemon and Olives. Chickpeas are often added to increase the protein content as quantities of meat used are usually small.

Couscous is the Berbers' most important contribution to Morocco's cooking. The light, elegant grain is the pasta of North Africa, and in Morocco it is eaten every Friday with a flavorsome stew such as Bedouin Chicken and Vegetable Couscous, and it also features on diffa (banquet) menus. The recipe for making couscous is given on page 54 for the curious, but few make it today as the process has been mechanised.

Lamb Soup with Chickpeas and Lentils, Harira, is the usual "break fast" meal during Ramadan, with bread, dates, milk and sweet fried dough. However, its popularity is such that it is sold as a street food year-round, ladled from cauldrons into earthenware bowls and sipped from lemonwood spoons.

Moroccan meals begin with cooling, refreshing salads or vegetables. Oranges feature when in season—Orange and Olive Salad and Orange Salad with Carrot are just two examples. A dusting of cinnamon or paprika, a scattering of cilantro (fresh coriander) leaves or nuts, a sprinkling of orange flower water—the cook creates according to ingredients on hand. Tomatoes, radishes, beets, cucumbers, red onions, bell peppers, eggplants—there is a wealth of ingredients available to Moroccan cooks to create the raw or cooked dishes that whet the appetite.

Meals finish with fresh fruit in season—at banquets these are beautifully displayed. At the end of a meal, mint tea is served, and if the occasion is special, sweet biscuits or pastries are offered—Nut Shortbread Cookies, Almond Pastry Snake and Gazelle's Horns are just three of them. For a very special occasion, a small glass of Almond Milk could be offered instead—this is one of the most delightful Moroccan sharbats, delicately flavored with rose water.

## ALGERIA

Algeria, Morocco and Tunisia are known as the Maghreb, Arabic for "west," and with Libya are known as the Greater Maghreb. In area, Algeria is the largest North African nation, but only one-fifth of its landmass is suitable for agriculture on the coastal strip, called the Tell. It was only after French colonization of Algeria that its borders were defined. While the French occupation might be cause for heated debate, since they left, Algeria now has to import some 60 percent of its food, whereas previously it was a food exporter. However, it is the largest producer of dates in the region, having many oases in the vast stretches of the Sahara.

Historically, Algeria's food mirrors that of Morocco as the Berber dynasties extended into present-day Morocco. However, names of certain ingredients and common dishes can vary. Warkha pastry is known as malsuqa (that which sticks), and is used for fried savory and sweet pastries. The soup eaten to break the fast during Ramadan is Chorba bil Lham, very similar to the Harira soup recipe on page 41.

One of the dishes that illustrates links to Morocco is Lamb Tagine with Dried Fruits. This rich meat dish, often served during Ramadan, shows the Persian influence on Arabic cooking—a similar dish is also prepared in Iraq.

The past French presence is evident in the bread of the cities. While the rural dweller will still make Country Bread, Kesra, and bake it in clay ovens, the city dwellers buy baguettes by the armful daily.

The Ottoman presence in coastal Algeria from the early sixteenth century until the French occupation is evident in the stuffed vegetable dishes that are prepared in Algeria. Vegetables stuffed with ground lamb, rice and spices are prepared more frequently here than elsewhere in the region. Ground Meat Kebabs and grilled lamb cubes on skewers are popular street foods.

Almost a million Algerian-born French were relocated to France; these people were known as pied-noirs in Algeria; in France they settled mostly in the South or in Paris. Their cooking is unique—a combination of French and Algerian, so if you visit an Algerian restaurant in France, ask if it is pied-noir cuisine or Algerian.

## TUNISIA

The smallest country in the region, Tunisia has a culinary history linked to ancient Carthage, Classical Greece, Imperial Rome, the Ottoman Empire and France. Many of its dishes are to be found in Moroccan cuisine, but it does have a few of its very own.

However, from a culinary point of view, it is better known for a condiment that is based on an ingredient from the New World—and that is harissa. This bitingly hot chili paste is to be found in almost every savory dish, and if not in the dish, it is on the table. Our recipe is a considerably toned-down version; if using harissa purchased in tubes or cans, add with caution.

Merguez, Spicy Lamb Sausage, contains harissa and other spices, and has been adopted by both Algerians and Moroccans. In all these countries it is a popular street food, grilled on a charcoal fire and served in bread with salad.

Brik is another Tunisian delicacy that is prepared in the other countries of the Maghreb. The pastry is malsuqa (Moroccan warkha) and the filling can contain a mixture of anchovies, tuna or cooked potato with onion, capers and herbs. A little filling is placed in the middle of a sheet of pastry, a hollow made and an egg broken into it. The pastry is turned over the filling, sealed and fried in hot oil. Spring roll wrappers can be used for the pastry; filo is not recommended as it is too fragile. This is a dish that should be eaten as soon as it is cooked, unless you prefer well-cooked egg, which wouldn't do in Tunisia.

Chakchouka, Peppers with Tomato and Eggs, is yet another Tunisian dish found in other cuisines—in Libya it is called shakshouka because of the dialectic differences in Arabic.

Bread, beverages, sweet pastries and puddings are similar to Morocco, including the presence of baguettes and croissants at bakeries and patisseries.

## LIBYA

After 300 years of Ottoman rule followed immediately by its colonization by Italy from 1911 to 1943, Libya's food is more a reflection of these influences rather than its proximity to Tunisia and Egypt. However, certain Egyptian dishes are very much a part of its culinary repertoire.

Agriculture and grazing lands are concentrated in the country's north coast; even then, in area these only comprise some 10 percent of Libya's landmass. Consequently Libya has to import many foods, and is able to do so because of its vast oil reserves. However the biggest problem is adequate fresh water.

The Italian influence is seen in the use of pasta and tomato paste in cooking, with some Italian-style breads in Libyan bakeries. Even though they use a lot of pasta, cheese is not used on it, and the sauces are meat- or chicken-based with onion, tomato paste and turmeric

and flat-leaf parsley if available. Penne is a favored pasta to serve with sauces, while orzo is used for soups.

Boureks are a legacy of the Ottomans, and are made with a yeast dough, a dough made with flour and olive oil, or imported puff pastry. Fillings can be of spinach, ground lamb with onion and spices, and canned tuna (imported) extended with hard-cooked eggs. The latter is simply called Thon Ajin—"ajin" is Arabic for dough.

Influences from Tunisia are also seen in the tagines and couscous dishes using lamb, chicken or fish, and in shakshouka, similar to the Tunisian Chakchouka, although lamb is included in the Libyan version. The special spice mix used for some tagines and couscous stews is called hararat—a mixture of nutmeg, cinnamon, turmeric, allspice and a little cayenne pepper. Rice is used more in Libya than in the neighboring countries to the west. The Egyptian influence can be seen in red lentils in soups, and fava (broad) beans in soups and purees, such as Fava Bean Soup, Ful Nabed, and Fava Bean Puree, Besara. Chickpeas are sometimes used as a meat extender as in the western countries of the region.

Patisseries sell French-style pastries and baklava is also made. The Egyptian Semolina Cake, Basbousa, and Date Filled Pastries, Magrood, finished in a syrup are two of the popular sweets.

Tea is the most popular drink, black and brewed with sugar, with Turkish-style coffee a close second. Alcoholic drinks are not allowed, so water and fruit juices are the usual drinks.

## EGYPT

With a history so ancient and so awesome in its magnificence, perhaps too much is expected of Egypt's foods. Events mid-nineteenth century saw a cosmopolitan Egypt emerge, with foods influenced by French, Italians, Turks and Greeks more than Arabs. However, the new Egypt has loosened her links with the West and regained her own national identity. Consequently food preferences have reverted to those linked with its past, retaining tradition.

Taking a broad look at Egyptian food, bread stands out as being the most important component of the Egyptian diet. Vendors, flat wicker baskets piled high with aish baladi and perched precariously on their heads, wind their way through the crowded streets of Cairo to their favorite selling spot. This is the flat bread of Egypt, usually made with a combination of all-purpose (plain) and whole-wheat flour with sufficient leavening to form a pocket and a soft crust, and a reminder of the role Ancient Egypt played in developing the staff of life.

Barley, millet and wheat were the principal grains of earliest civilizations. According to anthropologists studying evidence, bread baked during these times was hard and chewy. Barley and millet do not contain adequate amounts of the gluten-forming proteins essential to make a light-textured bread. Wheat on the other hand does contain these proteins, but their nature can be altered if heat is applied at the wrong stage of preparation. The early wheat strains had to be heated before threshing so that the husk could be removed, so destroying these essential properties in the grain and giving wheat bread characteristics similar to those made of barley and millet.

The Ancient Egyptians developed a strain of wheat that could be threshed without the preliminary heating, taking a giant step toward the improvement of bread. Whether by accident or by design, they also found a means to leaven bread made from this wheat. Owing to the shortage of the new grain, some centuries passed before leavened bread spread beyond Egypt.

Expatriate Egyptians, living in countries where vast varieties of food are available, still yearn for the bean dishes of their homeland. Simmered Ful Beans, Ful Medamis, would probably be preferred, if offered, to the most exquisite French culinary creation, as it evokes nostalgia. They remember the ful vendors of home, with huge idras of ful simmering day and night, ready to provide a satisfying breakfast in the morning, a midday meal, or just a snack at any time. For the making of Ful Medamis in the home, they have a small electric hotplate which plugs into the standard power point. This keeps a constant low heat and is just large enough to take a small idra. Similar foods that will equally stir the Egyptian far from home are Fava Bean Patties, Fava Bean Puree and Fava Bean Soup. A prized vegetable is bamia (okra), mostly favored in meat and vegetable stews.

Pigeons are highly regarded and bred for the table; the recipe for Roast Stuffed Chicken, Farroog Mahshi, can be used for four squabs (specially bred pigeons) in place of the chickens. The stuffing for this particular recipe is usually made with a green wheat called fireek, obtainable at Middle Eastern markets; however, coarse bulgur (burghul) can be substituted.

Western influence is still evident at the dining table of Egypt. The table is spread with a cloth and all the components of the meal are placed in their respective dishes and set on the table at the beginning of the meal. Individual plates or bowls are set out, with knives, forks and spoons. However, the fellahin (peasants) eat with fingers in the traditional Arabic manner as described earlier.

Favorite beverages are syrup flavored with rose water or tamarind syrup mixed with water, almond milk, and Turkish coffee.

# equipment

**BARRAHD** A Moroccan teapot with a bulbous body and domed lid finished with a pointed knob, and styled on the English "Manchester" design. Used for brewing the national beverage, mint tea, it can be silver-plate, stainless steel or aluminum.

**COUSCOUSSIER** A slightly bulbous, tall cooking pot with a steamer section on top for steaming couscous. Can be made of copper or aluminum. A large pot with a steamer on top can be used instead.

**G'SAA** A large, shallow wooden or earthenware bowl in which bread dough is kneaded or couscous grains made. Also used for soaking couscous before steaming, and for rubbing and separating the grains during and after cooking.

**MORTAR AND PESTLE** Made of brass, these are used to pound whole spices, almonds and other ingredients that require pulverizing.

**TAGINE** A shallow, glazed earthenware cooking pot with a distinctive, conical lid; also the name of the dish cooked in it. Berber in origin, it is placed over a charcoal brazier. However, a saucepan is more likely to be used today, with the food transferred to the tagine for serving.

**TANGIA** A Moroccan urn-shaped earthenware cooking pot in which ingredients are placed, with parchment tied on top to seal. It is taken to the local bathhouse boiler room and placed in the embers to cook slowly for several hours. The food cooked in this pot is also called tangia.

**TOBSIL DEL WARKHA** A round pan usually about 12–14 in (30–35 cm) in diameter and 2 in (5 cm) deep, made of tin-coated copper. It is upturned over a gas flame, charcoal brazier or a pan of boiling water for making warkha pastry (see Ingredients, page 15).

**Couscoussier**

**Tagine**

# ingredients

**ALMONDS** Used for sweet and savory dishes, whole, chopped or ground to an almond meal. If ground almonds are unavailable, use dry, crisp whole or slivered almonds and grind to a meal in a food processor or nut grinder. When using cup measures, pack well as processed almonds are lighter in texture than commercially-ground almond meal. For example 1 cup processed almonds is lighter than 1 cup ground almonds/almond meal, unless packed well.

**CHICKPEAS** The most popular pulse in the region, they are mainly used to add extra food value to tagines and couscous as often only a small amount of meat or poultry is used. Dried chickpeas are soaked overnight and added to the pot with the main ingredients, allowing 1½–2 hours cooking; however, canned chickpeas are more convenient.

**CILANTRO (FRESH CORIANDER)** Essential in North African cooking, cilantro (fresh coriander) has feathery green leaves with a somewhat pungent aroma and flavor that nevertheless complements spicy foods.

**CINNAMON** Used for both savory and sweet dishes, either ground or as sticks or quills about 3 in (7.5 cm) long. Cassia is related to cinnamon and also used; the bark comes in thickish shards or is made into quills and often sold as cinnamon.

**CORIANDER** The seeds of the cilantro (fresh coriander) plant are dried, ground and used as a spice, having a flavor similar to a combination of lemon zest and sage.

**COUSCOUS** Originating with the Berbers of North Africa, couscous is made into tiny pellets by rolling semolina grains with durum wheat flour, salt and water. Finely-cracked barley and maize are also used as a couscous.

**CUMIN** With a warm, sweet aroma, yet pungent and earthy, cumin is one of the most popular spices in the region. Select a darker cumin with a greenish-brown color for best flavor, or use freshly-ground seeds.

**FAVA (BROAD) BEAN** Dried beans are soaked for 48 hours and the leathery skin removed for making bessara and tameya. Tear skin with the point of a knife or fingernail, squeeze and bean pops out. Middle Eastern markets have dried, ready-skinned fava beans; soak these for 12 hours.

**FILO** Also known as phyllo or fillo, this pastry of Greek/Middle Eastern origins is made of a flour dough and machine-rolled to tissue-paper thinness. Available fresh chilled or frozen; use as a substitute for warkha pastry, it can be baked as well as fried. Thaw frozen filo in the refrigerator; leave thawed frozen or fresh chilled filo at room temperature, in its packaging, for 1–2 hours before attempting to open out the sheets.

**FUL MEDAMIS BEAN** A variety of fava (broad) bean used in Egypt for the national dish of the same name. It is like a small, fat fava bean, ranging in color from beige to purple-brown. It has the characteristic black dot but has a thinner skin which is not removed for cooking. Available at Middle Eastern markets and some health food stores.

**GHEE** Known as smen, samen and samn in the regional dialects, this form of butter has the milk solids removed and can be kept at room temperature. Available in food stores, but check label to ensure it is pure butterfat, as other fats are sometimes included.

**LENTILS** The brown/green European lentils are the most popular in the region. In Egypt they also use the tiny red lentils, which have a spicy flavor. Lentils do not require presoaking.

**MASTIC** A resin from a small evergreen tree that grows in regions of the Mediterranean, especially the Greek island of Chios. Used to flavor baked goods, but in Egypt, a little is used when boiling lamb to improve its aroma.

**MELOKHIA** A secondary source of jute grown in Egypt, where the young stalks are harvested, stripped of their leaves and used as a pot herb for a soup of the same name. It is favored for its viscous properties. Sometimes available fresh, but the dried leaves can be found at Middle Eastern markets.

**MINT** Fresh mint is used occasionally in cooking, or scattered over salads and fruit desserts. However, its principle use, especially in Morocco, is for mint tea. Spearmint (*Mentha spicata*) is the variety used.

**OLIVE OIL** Olive oil is used for salads, but there is an increasing trend in the region to replace ghee in cooking with olive or other oil in the interests of better health. Use extra virgin olive oil for salads and standard olive oil for cooking, although other vegetable oils are also used.

**ORANGE FLOWER WATER** Made from distilled blossoms of the bitter orange, originating in the Middle East and introduced to North Africa by the Arabs. Used to flavor beverages and sweet and savory foods.

**PAPRIKA** The paprika most commonly used in the region is Spanish mild paprika. It is used as much for its color as its flavor.

**PARSLEY** Flat-leaf or Italian parsley is used. If you cannot obtain this variety, use curly-leafed parsley and include some of the stalks when chopping to increase its flavor.

**ROSE WATER** Made from distilled fragrant rose petals, originating in Persia and introduced to North Africa by the Arabs. Used to flavor beverages and sweet and savory foods.

**SAFFRON** The dried stigmas of *Crocus sativus*. Introduced by the Arabs, it is grown in Morocco. Threads and powdered saffron are widely used for flavor and color. Only a little is required to impart its magical color and aroma.

**SEMOLINA** Fine to coarse grains milled from the inner endosperm of durum wheat, beige in color. Outside the region, it is generally sold as a breakfast cereal (cream of wheat); do not confuse with semolina flour made from durum wheat for pasta-making. Used in baking and is the basis for couscous.

**TARO (*Colocasia esculenta*)** A large, starchy tuber used in Egypt where it is known as kolkas. The root must be washed and dried before peeling as it becomes slimy if washed after peeling. It is toxic when raw.

**WARKHA/OURKA** (Morocco); **MALSUQA** (Algeria/Tunisia) This tissue-thin pastry is still hand-made in the Maghreb. Dough is tapped repeatedly on an up-turned, heated tin-lined copper container until its surface is covered, with the sheet of pastry lifted off when it dries. Used for Chicken and Almond Pie, Bisteeya, and other pastries. Recipes using warkha are never baked, only fried. Filo pastry or spring roll wrappers are good substitutes.

# Preserved lemons Hamad m'rakhad
## MOROCCO

**Select fresh firm lemons with no blemishes. In Morocco, they use the fragrant lemon called doqq (the Meyer lemon), and the more tart boussera. Eureka, Lisbon or Villa Franca lemons may be used providing their skins are not too thick. Ripe (yellow) limes may also be used.**

Choose jars which will take amount of lemons to be salted; a capacity of 2 cups (16 fl oz/500 ml) is recommended, and will take 2 lemons, plus extra peels. Measure capacity of each jar. Sterilize jars and plastic lids by boiling. For each 1-cup (8-fl oz/250-ml) capacity, you will need 5 level teaspoons (1 oz/30 g) kosher salt.

Wash lemons and wipe dry with a clean cloth. If very firm, soak lemons in cold water for 3 days to soften them, changing water daily.

Measure out salt required for each jar and set it aside with its jar. Halve and juice 3 lemons to begin. Strain juice and cut lemon skins in half (these can also be preserved). More lemons can be juiced as required. Cut lemons to be preserved almost through into quarters from stem end, leaving them joined at the base.

Pack one jar at a time: sprinkle cut surfaces of lemons with some of salt allocated to their jar, and press lemons back into shape. Place about 1 tablespoon of remaining salt into base of jar. Add 1 lemon, fill spaces with 2–3 pieces of peel, and sprinkle with a little more salt. Add another lemon and more peel to fill spaces, squashing the whole lemons as much as possible into the jar so they may release their juice. Fill jar in this manner. Add any remaining salt, half-fill jar with strained lemon juice, and fill to top with cooled, boiled water. Place a piece of lemon peel on top, then seal tightly with plastic lid. Jar should be filled to capacity with lemons, lemon peels and liquid.

Wipe outside of jar and store in a cool, dark cupboard; occasionally tilt jars back and forth for first 3–4 days to dissolve salt. Preserved lemons will be ready to use in 4 weeks, and will keep for up to 6 months.

NOTE: If any mold does form, it will do so on the piece of lemon peel on top—simply skim off mold and discard the piece of peel. Do not add any oil to jar. Once jar is opened, store in refrigerator.

TO USE: Using a clean fork, remove lemon to a clean plate, cut amount required then return any remaining lemon to jar and reseal. Discard all pulp and membrane from lemon, leaving peel with pith intact. Rinse peel well under cold water and chop, dice or slice as directed in recipes.

# Spice blend
## Ras el hanout
MOROCCO, ALGERIA
TUNISIA

There is some difference between the blends of the different countries; in fact there are differences between blends from different spice shops. For example, Tunisian blends contain more chili than those of the other countries. Use the freshest possible spices.

**Makes** 1½ oz (45 g)

3 teaspoons freshly-grated nutmeg
3 teaspoons ground coriander
3 teaspoons ground cumin
2 teaspoons ground allspice
2 teaspoons ground ginger
2 teaspoons ground cumin
1½ teaspoons ground cardamom
1 teaspoon freshly-ground black pepper
½ teaspoon ground cloves
¼ teaspoon cayenne pepper

Place all spices in a bowl and mix thoroughly. Transfer to a jar, seal and store in a cool, dark place. Use as directed in recipes; or add to game dishes, tagines of fish, lamb or beef that contain fruit or honey, or sweet stews served with couscous.

# Seed and spice blend
## Dukkah
EGYPT

**Makes** 1¾ cups (8 oz/250 g)

⅔ cup (3 oz/90 g) sesame seeds
½ cup (2½ oz/75 g) toasted hazelnuts
⅓ cup (1½ oz/45 g) coriander seeds
¼ cup (1 oz/30 g) cumin seeds
about 1 teaspoon sea salt
½ teaspoon freshly-ground black pepper

Place sesame seeds in a heavy-based, dry frying pan over medium heat and stir often until lightly toasted. Tip immediately into a bowl to prevent them overbrowning and set aside to cool.

Chop hazelnuts coarsely. Pound or grind coriander seeds and cumin seeds to a coarse powder.

When sesame seeds are cool, add hazelnuts, coriander and cumin, salt to taste and pepper to bowl. Mix well then place in a food processor and process just long enough to break up some of sesame seeds and chop nuts a little more, about 30 seconds. Do not overprocess or mixture will become oily. It must be a dry mixture.

Serve required amount of dukkah in a shallow bowl and provide sliced breads (thick, Egyptian flat breads, Turkish pide bread, or baguette) and a shallow bowl of olive oil. Bread is dipped into oil, then into dukkah and eaten as an appetizer. Store remaining dukkah in a sealed jar in a cool, dark place.

NOTE: Toasted hazelnuts are available in gourmet food stores and specialist nut shops. Otherwise toast hazelnuts on a baking sheet in a preheated oven at 350°F (180°C/Gas 4) for 10 minutes and rub off skins in a kitchen towel.

# Basic couscous Seksu
## MOROCCO

**Serves** 6

2½ cups (1 lb/500 g) instant couscous
2½ cups (20 fl oz/625 ml) water
1 teaspoon salt
⅓ cup (3 oz/90 g) butter

Place couscous in a baking dish. Place water, salt and 2 tablespoons butter in a saucepan and bring to a boil. Pour boiling water evenly over couscous. Spread couscous evenly, cover with baking sheet or aluminum foil, and let stand 5 minutes. Stir with a fork, cover and let stand a further 5 minutes. Stir with fork and separate any lumps with your fingers.

To heat, choose a steamer or metal colander which fits snugly over pan of food being cooked or boiling water and line with a piece of muslin (cheesecloth). Drape long piece of aluminum foil around rim of pan, fit steamer into place on pan, and scrunch foil to seal. Spread couscous evenly in steamer, and steam over boiling water or other ingredients until steam rises through couscous grains, about 20 minutes, occasionally forking it lightly so that it heats evenly.

Meanwhile, melt remaining butter. When couscous is hot, transfer to heated platter, pour over melted butter and fork it through. Pile up and serve immediately.

See Couscous (page 54) for couscous grains made in the traditional way.

# Charmoula Chermoula
## MOROCCO

**Serves** 6

¼ Preserved Lemon (page 16)
2 cloves garlic
3 tablespoons chopped cilantro (fresh coriander) leaves
3 tablespoons chopped fresh flat-leaf (Italian) parsley
⅛ teaspoon powdered saffron (optional)
½ teaspoon paprika
⅛–¼ teaspoon cayenne pepper
½ teaspoon ground cumin
½ teaspoon salt
2 tablespoons lemon juice
4 tablespoons olive oil

Discard pulp from preserved lemon, rinse peel and pat dry. Place peel with remaining ingredients in a food processor and process to a coarse puree. Use as a marinade or baste for fish and seafood, or as directed in recipes.

# Hot pepper sauce
## Harissa
TUNISIA

This fiery condiment is used widely in Tunisian cooking, and has crossed borders to Algeria and Morocco. It is available in tubes and cans at some specialty-food stores; if using commercially-prepared harissa, add with caution to recipes as it is much hotter than the version given below. While most versions call for dried chilies or hot chili or cayenne pepper, make it with fresh red chili whenever possible. Because chilies come in many varieties and sizes, I have given weight as an indication. If you can tolerate very hot condiments, use the whole chilies; otherwise remove seeds as their inclusion increases the fieriness of the finished harissa. When handling fresh chilies, do not touch eyes or mouth as they can be very irritating and wash hands immediately after preparation.

**Makes** ½ cup (4 fl oz/125 ml)

1 whole or 4 tablespoons chopped canned pimiento
2 oz (60 g) fresh hot red chilies or 3 teaspoons dried red chili
   pepper flakes
½ teaspoon salt
3 cloves garlic, chopped
1 teaspoon ground coriander
1 teaspoon ground cumin
olive oil (optional)

If using whole canned pimiento, drain well and pat dry with paper towels. Remove seeds from fresh chilies, removing membranes if desired, and chop roughly.

   Place chili, pimiento, salt, garlic, coriander and cumin in a food processor and process to a finely-textured, thick puree. Use immediately as directed in recipes, or transfer to a sterilized jar, cover with a film of olive oil, seal and store in the refrigerator for up to 2 weeks.

# Garlic sauce
## Ta'leya I
EGYPT

This is more of a condiment to be added to cooked dishes than a sauce, and is a somewhat modified version—in Egypt, usually 6 or 7 garlic cloves are used for adding to a dish serving six. As garlic increases in pungency when cooked, decrease amount further if you wish. Of course the result depends on size and pungency of garlic cloves used.

3–4 cloves garlic
¼ teaspoon salt
2 tablespoons ghee or butter
1 teaspoon ground coriander
pinch cayenne pepper

Crush garlic with salt in a mortar using a pestle. Alternatively crush in a garlic press and mix with salt.
   Heat ghee or butter in a small saucepan and add garlic. Cook, stirring constantly, until golden-brown. Remove pan from heat and stir in coriander and pepper. Use while sizzling hot, as directed in recipes.

# Onion sauce
## Ta'leya II
EGYPT

¼ cup (2 fl oz/60 ml) olive oil
2 large onions
1–2 cloves garlic, finely chopped

Peel onions and cut in half lengthwise then slice thinly into semicircles.
   Heat olive oil in a frying pan, add onions and fry over medium heat until golden-brown. Add garlic and cook for a further 1 minute. Use as directed in recipes.

**Pictured right (from front): Hot Pepper Sauce, Onion Sauce, Garlic Sauce, Charmoula.**

# Sesame bread rings Semit

## EGYPT

**Makes** about 18
**Cooking time** 15 minutes

2½ teaspoons or ¼-oz (7-g) sachet active dry
   yeast
2 teaspoons sugar
¾ cup (6 fl oz/180 ml) lukewarm water
4 cups (20 oz/600 g) all-purpose (plain) flour
1 teaspoon salt
½ cup (4 fl oz/125 ml) milk, boiled and cooled
   to lukewarm
2 teaspoons oil
sesame seeds
1 small egg, beaten

Place yeast and sugar in a bowl with
¼ cup (2 fl oz/60 ml) lukewarm water and
dissolve. Sift flour and salt into a mixing
bowl, remove about 1 cup (5 oz/150 g)
flour and set aside.

Add remaining water and warm milk to
yeast. Pour liquid into center of flour and
stir in a little of flour to thicken liquid.
Cover and let stand in a warm place until
frothy, about 10 minutes. Mix remaining
flour with liquid in bowl and beat until
smooth, then beat by hand for 10 minutes
or using an electric mixer with dough hook
for 5 minutes.

Gradually beat in oil, then knead or beat
in as much of reserved flour as dough will
take, until dough is smooth and satiny,
5–10 minutes. Cover tightly with plastic
wrap and set aside in a warm place until
doubled in bulk, about 30 minutes.

Punch down dough and turn out onto a
lightly floured board. Knead a little, then
break off pieces the size of a small egg.
Place sesame seeds in a small plate.
Lightly oil a baking sheet.

Roll 1 piece of dough into a rope ½ in
(1 cm) thick and 8 in (20 cm) long. Form
into a ring, overlapping ends and pressing
to join. Repeat to make about 5 rings.
Glaze with beaten egg, dip tops in sesame
seeds then place on baking sheet. Repeat
to make remaining dough into rings, about
5 at a time. Cover finished semit with a
cloth and set aside in a draught-free place
until doubled in size, about 30 minutes.

Preheat oven to 425°F (220°C/Gas 7).
Place a baking dish of hot water on bottom
shelf of oven. Place semit on center shelf
and bake until semit sounds hollow when
tapped, about 15 minutes. When cooked,
brush semit while hot with water and let
cool on baking sheets: this crisps the crust.

NOTE: Normally each semit is made
separately, but preparing them in small
batches speeds up the job. However, if you
shape all of them before glazing, the first
begin to rise and they are more difficult to
handle so keep batches small.

VARIATION: EGYPTIAN PITA BREAD (AISH
BALADI) Follow recipe for Country Bread
(page 23) using half all-purpose (plain)
flour and half whole-wheat (wholemeal)
flour. Rise dough in a covered bowl, punch
down and divide into 8 portions. On a
floured work surface, roll each portion into
a ball then into a 7-in (18-cm) round. Set
aside on kitchen towels for 10 minutes.
Preheat oven to 500°F (250°C/Gas 10) and
preheat baking sheets. Bake on hot baking
sheets until bread is puffed and sounds
hollow when tapped, about 4–5 minutes.
Remove from oven, wrap bread in a
kitchen towel and set aside to cool.

# Country bread Kesra
## MOROCCO, ALGERIA, TUNISIA

**Makes** 2 loaves
**Cooking time** 12–15 minutes

2½ **teaspoons or ¼-oz (7-g) sachet active dry yeast**
1½ **cups (12 fl oz/375 ml) lukewarm water**
4 **cups (20 oz/600 g) plain (all-purpose) flour, preferably unbleached**
1 **teaspoon salt**
2 **tablespoons semolina or polenta**

1 **tablespoon toasted sesame seeds, whole aniseed, or flaked sea salt for topping breads (optional)**

Dissolve yeast in ½ cup (4 fl oz/125 ml) lukewarm water. Sift flours and salt into a mixing bowl and make a well in center. Pour in yeast mixture and remaining water. Stir a little of flour into yeast mixture, cover and set aside in a warm place until frothy, about 10 minutes.

Mix to a soft dough, adding a little extra water if dough is too firm. Turn out onto a lightly floured work surface and knead until smooth and elastic and dough springs back when pressed with fingertip, about 10 minutes. Only add extra flour if dough remains sticky after a few minutes of kneading.

As this bread requires only one rising, halve dough and shape each portion into a ball. Roll out on lightly floured work surface to 9-in (23-cm) rounds or 11-in (28-cm) rounds for thinner breads.

Sift semolina or polenta onto baking trays. Lift rounds onto trays, reshaping if necessary. Brush tops lightly with water and, if desired, sprinkle with choice of topping, pressing in lightly. Cover loaves with kitchen towels and set aside in a warm, draught-free place for 1 hour to rise: bread is ready when a depression remains when pressed lightly with fingertip.

While loaves are rising, preheat oven to 425°F (220°C/Gas 7). Just before baking, prick thinner breads in several places with a fork. Bake until loaves are golden and sound hollow when tops are tapped with a wooden spoon, 12–15 minutes.

Let cool on a wire rack and use on day of baking, or wrap well and freeze. The thicker loaves are traditionally cut in wedges to serve.

NOTE: Bread may be made in an electric bread maker using Dough setting, removing dough before rising begins, or use an electric mixer with a dough hook; add ingredients, except topping, all together in order given.

# Marinated olives

Adding flavorings to olives makes them even more appealing as appetizers. While many are available already marinated, it is easy to make your own. Here are some ways in which cured olives are prepared in various countries of the region. Rinse all olives and drain well before preparing.

## TUNISIA

1 lb (500 g) black or green olives
2 teaspoons Harissa (page 20)
½ cup (4 fl oz/125 ml) olive oil

Mix olives with harissa and oil. Place in a jar, seal and refrigerate for 1–2 days before using. Bring to room temperature before serving. Olives can be stored in refrigerator for up to 1 month, shaking jar occasionally to distribute marinade.

## MOROCCO

1 lb (500 g) black, purple or green olives
2 tablespoons finely-chopped fresh flat-leaf (Italian) parsley
2 tablespoons finely-chopped cilantro (fresh coriander) leaves
2 cloves garlic, finely chopped
1 tablespoon finely-chopped Preserved Lemon rind (page 16)
1 teaspoon finely-chopped fresh hot red chili
½ teaspoon ground cumin
1 tablespoon juice from Preserved Lemon jar
2 tablespoons fresh lemon juice
½ cup (4 fl oz/125 ml) olive oil

Place all ingredients in a bowl and mix well. Transfer to jar, seal and refrigerate for 1–2 days. Bring to room temperature before serving.

VARIATION: If you do not have preserved lemons, use 2 teaspoons finely-shredded fresh orange zest (no pith) and increase fresh lemon juice to 3 tablespoons.

# Tahini salad Salata tahina

## EGYPT

**Makes** about 1¾ cups

2 cloves garlic
salt
¾ cup (6 fl oz/180 ml) tahini
1 tablespoon white vinegar
juice of 1 lemon
½ cup (4 fl oz/125 ml) water
½ teaspoon ground cumin
½ cup (¾ oz/20 g) chopped fresh flat-leaf
  (Italian) parsley

Crush garlic cloves with ½ teaspoon salt.

Place tahini in a mixing bowl and beat well. This preliminary beating reduces the strong flavor of the tahini.

Beat in garlic and vinegar. Gradually beat in lemon juice alternately with water. To ensure a good creamy consistency, add enough lemon juice to make tahini very thick before adding water: this gives you more scope in adjusting the flavor and texture.

Add salt to taste, and more lemon juice if a sharper sauce is required. Mix in cumin and parsley, and refrigerate to chill until required. Serve as an appetizer, or as directed in recipes.

# Chickpea and tahini dip
# Hummus bi tahini
## EGYPT

To make this in the traditional way, soak 1 cup (7 oz/220 g) dried chickpeas in 3 cups (24 fl oz/750 ml) water for 12 hours in the refrigerator. Purists would remove the fine skins from the chickpeas but this is not necessary. If you do want to skin them, place soaked dried chickpeas in a large quantity of cold water. Rub handfuls of the peas together, drop them back in the water and repeat (removing skins as they accumulate on top of the water). Then, to cook, simply drain the chickpeas and boil in water to cover (no salt) until very soft, 1½–2 hours. This dip keeps for several days in the refrigerator.

**Makes** about 3 cups (24 fl oz/750 ml)

two 14-oz (425-g) cans chickpeas
2 cloves garlic, chopped
juice of 1 lemon
½ cup (4 fl oz/125 ml) tahini
½ teaspoon ground cumin
pinch cayenne pepper
salt
olive oil and paprika for garnish
Egyptian Pita Bread (page 22) or other pita
    bread for serving

Drain chickpeas, reserving liquid and 3 or 4 whole chickpeas. Place in a food processor with garlic and process to a smooth puree, adding a little lemon juice. Add tahini, cumin and cayenne pepper, and process, adding more lemon juice. When mixture becomes too thick to process, add about 3 tablespoons reserved chickpea liquid; consistency should be thick but creamy. Check flavor, and add more lemon juice if necessary and salt to taste. Transfer to bowl, cover and refrigerate until required.

To serve, place hummus in shallow dish. Drizzle with olive oil and dust with paprika. Garnish with reserved chickpeas, and serve with bread.

# Simmered ful beans Ful medamis
## EGYPT

Ful, ful medamis, faba, tic, Egyptian brown—these are the various names used for this most ancient of beans, popular in Egypt for centuries, perhaps from the time of the Pharaohs. The beans look like small, rounded fava (broad) beans and can be found in Middle Eastern and Greek markets; fava beans cannot be substituted as their flavor is too strong.

Long, slow cooking is required; indeed in Egypt, where ful medamis is the national dish, purveyors simmer their beans overnight so that they are ready for the early morning customers. The lemon juice and olive oil are added to taste, and the beans are eaten with accompaniments of choice.

**Serves** 6

2 cups (13 oz/400 g) ful medamis beans
6 cups (48 fl oz/1.5 L) water
¼ cup (1½ oz/45 g) red lentils
salt
3 cloves garlic, crushed
½ teaspoon ground cumin

For serving:
finely-chopped fresh flat-leaf (Italian) parsley
lemon wedges
freshly-ground black pepper
1 quantity Tahini Salad (page 26) (optional)
romaine (cos) lettuce leaves
sliced tomato and cucumber
6 hard-cooked (boiled) eggs (optional)
Egyptian Pita Bread (page 22) or other pita bread
olive oil

Place beans in sieve and pick over to remove any extra matter. Rinse under cold running water. Place in bowl with 6 cups (48 fl oz/1.5 L) water, cover and soak overnight in refrigerator.

Transfer beans and their soaking water to large saucepan. Place lentils in sieve and pick over to remove any extra matter. Rinse under cold running water and add to saucepan with beans. Bring slowly to a boil, cover pan and simmer over very low heat until beans are very tender, about 5–6 hours: do not stir while cooking or beans will stick to saucepan. Stir in salt to taste, garlic and cumin.

To serve, spoon hot beans into wide soup bowls or pasta plates and sprinkle with parsley. Serve with lemon wedges, black pepper, Tahini Salad, lettuce, tomato, cucumber, eggs and bread placed in bowls and dishes, and a small pitcher of olive oil.

VARIATION: FUL MEDAMIS MAZZA (PUREED FUL BEANS) Puree 2 cups cooked ful beans with their liquid. Let cool and add olive oil and lemon juice to taste. Swirl puree into shallow dish, drizzle with a little olive oil and sprinkle with chopped fresh parsley. Serve with pita bread.

# Eggplant jam Batenjel m'charmel
## ALGERIA

**Serves** 6–8
**Cooking time** 25–30 minutes

1½ lb (750 g) long thin (Japanese) eggplants
 (aubergines)
olive oil for frying
2 cloves garlic, crushed
1 teaspoon paprika
1 teaspoon ground cumin
⅛–¼ teaspoon cayenne pepper
2 tablespoons finely-chopped cilantro (fresh
 coriander)
sea salt and freshly-ground black pepper
1–2 tablespoons lemon juice

1 tablespoon finely-chopped fresh flat-leaf
 (Italian) parsley for garnish
extra paprika for garnish
lemon slices for garnish

Wash eggplants, cut off stems and using a vegetable peeler, remove ½-in (12-mm) strips of skin along the length of each eggplant to reduce skin content of jam. Cut eggplants lengthwise in ½-in (12-mm) slices. Long eggplants do not require salting.

Heat oil to a depth of ¼ in (5 mm) in a frying pan and, working in batches, fry eggplant slices until browned on each side and tender, adding more oil to pan as needed. Remove using a slotted spoon and let cool slightly, reserving oil in pan. Cut cooked eggplant slices in half lengthwise, then cut into dice.

Reduce heat to low, and add garlic, paprika, cumin and cayenne pepper to oil in pan. Cook, stirring, for 30 seconds. Add chopped eggplant and cilantro, increase heat to medium, and cook, stirring often, until most of moisture has evaporated and mixture has a jam-like consistency. Drain off excess oil, but leave some in as it contributes to flavor. Stir in salt, pepper and lemon juice to taste.

Transfer to a bowl, sprinkle with chopped parsley and a dusting of paprika, and garnish with lemon slices. Serve at room temperature with pita bread.

# Fava bean puree Besara
## EGYPT

Large dried fava or broad beans (ful nabed) are used for besara. Those sold skinless are cream in color and though not readily available, are well worth using if you can find them. Soak skinned beans for 24 hours in a cold place. Beans with skin intact require longer soaking so that the tough skin can be removed (see Ingredients, page 14).

The melokhia in the recipe is optional; its use imparts a green color to the puree without affecting the flavor. Use a large stainless steel or an enameled cast iron utensil for cooking.

**Serves** 5–6
**Cooking time** 1¼–1½ hours

2 cups (12 oz/375 g) dried fava (broad) beans or
    1½ cups (9 oz/280 g) ready-skinned dried
    beans
cold water
salt and freshly-ground black pepper
2 teaspoons dried mint
1 teaspoon dried melokhia (optional)

For serving:
Onion Sauce (page 20)
olive oil
chopped onions
lemon wedges

Cover beans well with cold water and let soak for 48 hours, skinned beans for 24 hours, changing water 2 or 3 times. Drain beans and remove skins if present (see page 14).

Place prepared beans in a saucepan with water to cover and bring to a slow simmer. Cover and simmer gently until very soft, about 1½ hours.

Puree cooked beans in a blender or press through a sieve using a wooden spoon, and return to pan. Add salt and pepper to taste, mint rubbed to a powder, and well-rubbed melokhia if using. Cook gently, uncovered, until bubbling.

Serve hot in small bowls, garnishing each with Onion Sauce. Place a cruet of olive oil, chopped onions and lemon wedges in bowls at the table, to be added to taste. Serve with pita or crusty bread.

# Fava bean patties Tameya

## EGYPT

**Makes** 30
**Cooking time** 5 minutes each batch

2 cups (12 oz/375 g) dried fava (broad) beans or
  1½ cups (9 oz/280 g) ready-skinned dried
  beans
water
1 cup (3 oz/90 g) chopped scallions
  (shallots/spring onions)
¼ cup (⅓ oz/10 g) chopped fresh flat-leaf
  (Italian) parsley
2 tablespoons chopped cilantro (fresh
  coriander) leaves
3 cloves garlic
1½ teaspoons salt
freshly-ground black pepper
¼ teaspoon cayenne pepper
¼ teaspoon baking soda

sesame seeds (optional)
oil for deep frying

Cover beans well with cold water and let soak for 48 hours, skinned beans for 24 hours, changing water 2 or 3 times. Drain beans and remove skins if present (see page 14).

Mix uncooked prepared beans in a bowl with scallions, parsley, cilantro, garlic, salt, black pepper, cayenne pepper and baking soda. Working in 2 batches, process in a food processor until finely ground then remove to a bowl. Knead mixture in bowl to a paste and let stand for 30 minutes.

With wet hands, take about 1 tablespoon of mixture at a time and shape into thick patties about 1½ in (4 cm) in diameter. Dip each side in sesame seeds if using. Place on a tray and let stand at room temperature for 20 minutes.

Heat oil for deep frying to 350°F (180°C) or until a cube of bread turns golden in 15 seconds. Add tameya, a few at a time, and cook until deep golden-brown, turning to brown evenly, about 5 minutes. Remove using a slotted spoon and drain on paper towels.

Serve hot with Tahini Salad (page 26), and assorted salad vegetables such as tomato, cucumber, bell peppers (capsicums) and lettuce.

VARIATION: TRADITIONAL METHOD
Pass beans twice through a food grinder using a fine screen. Mix with remaining ingredients and pass through grinder twice more. Knead to a paste and shape and cook as in recipe above.

# Spinach pastries Bourek

LIBYA

**Makes** 32
**Cooking time** 25 minutes, including filling

1 quantity Country Bread dough (page 23)
two 8-oz (250-g) packages frozen leaf spinach,
   thawed
¼ cup (2 fl oz/60 ml) olive oil
1 onion, finely chopped
2 tablespoons chopped fresh dill
¾ cup (4 oz/125 g) crumbled feta cheese
salt and freshly-ground black pepper
1 egg beaten with 1 tablespoon milk

Make bread dough according to directions on page 23, cover and let rise until doubled in bulk, either in mixing bowl or bread maker.

Meanwhile, drain thawed spinach in a sieve, pressing it well with the back of a spoon to remove moisture. Heat oil in a frying pan, add onion and cook over low heat until translucent. Transfer to a bowl and add spinach and dill. Mix in feta cheese and season to taste with salt and pepper. Divide into 4 portions.

When dough has risen, knock down and turn out onto a lightly-floured work surface. Knead lightly and divide into 4 equal portions, rolling each into a ball. Cover with a cloth. Roll out 1 ball of dough into a rectangle about 20 in (50 cm) long and 5½ in (14 cm) wide. Using one portion of filling, spread along center of dough in a 2½-in (6-cm) wide strip. Fold sides of dough over filling and press ends to seal. Turn dough strip over and trim ends. Place filled dough, seam-side down, onto a greased baking sheet, halving strip if too long. Repeat with remaining dough and filling.

Using a sharp knife, cut each strip through to base in approximately 2½-in (6-cm) squares. Cover with a dry cloth and let rise in a warm place for 20 minutes. Preheat oven to 400°F (200°C/Gas 6).

Brush tops of pastries with beaten egg and bake until golden and pastries sound hollow when tapped, about 15 minutes. Remove to a cutting board and cut through to separate into individual pastries. Serve hot or warm.

# Fried pastries with meat filling
## Briouats bil lham
### MOROCCO, ALGERIA, TUNISIA

**Makes** about 48
**Cooking time** 25–30 minutes for filling,
1–2 minutes per batch for frying

1 tablespoon oil
1 medium onion, finely chopped
2 cloves garlic, crushed
2 teaspoons ground cumin
1 teaspoon ground ginger
½ teaspoon ground turmeric
½ teaspoon paprika
¼–½ teaspoon cayenne pepper
1 lb (500 g) finely-ground (minced) lamb or beef
½ cup (4 fl oz/125 ml) water
salt and freshly-ground black pepper
2 tablespoons chopped cilantro (fresh
  coriander)
2 tablespoons chopped fresh flat-leaf (Italian)
  parsley

8 sheets filo (phyllo) pastry
1 egg white, beaten
oil for frying

In a frying pan, with lid to fit, heat oil and gently cook onion until translucent. Add garlic, cumin, ginger, turmeric, paprika and cayenne pepper to taste, and cook, stirring, for 30 seconds. Add ground meat and cook over high heat, stirring often to break up lumps. When crumbly, reduce heat, stir in water and salt and pepper to taste, cover and simmer over low heat for 15 minutes. Stir in herbs and cook, uncovered, until moisture evaporates. Remove pan from heat and set aside to cool.

Stack filo on a cutting board with longer side toward you. Using a ruler and craft knife, cut sheets crosswise into strips 2½ in (6 cm) wide and 11–12 in (28–30 cm) long. Stack strips in folds of a dry kitchen towel.

Place 1 filo strip on work surface with short end toward you. Put 1 heaping teaspoon meat filling ¾-in (2-cm) in from base of strip and fold end diagonally across filling so that base lines up with side of strip, forming a triangle. Fold straight up once, then fold diagonally to opposite side. Complete folding in the same manner until near end of strip, then lightly brush end of filo with egg white and complete fold. Place sealed-side down on a cloth-covered tray. Repeat with remaining ingredients and cover with a kitchen towel until ready to fry; these must be cooked within 10 minutes of shaping.

Heat oil to a depth of ½ in (1 cm) in a frying pan over medium heat. When oil is hot but not fuming, add pastries, 6–8 at a time, and cook until crisp and golden. Remove with a slotted spoon and drain on paper towels. Repeat to cook remaining pastries. Serve hot.

# soups

## Green herb soup Melokhia
### EGYPT

Though in Egypt a stock made from any available vegetables is often used, it is preferable to have a meat stock base. This can be from lamb, beef or chicken. If chicken is used, the bird is roasted with butter after the initial boiling and served separately as part of the meal. Egyptians living abroad find our mass-produced chickens lack flavor, and many add a stock cube so that the end result is just like "back home." For more information on melokhia, see Ingredients.

**Serves** 6
**Cooking time** 15–20 minutes

6 cups (48 fl oz/1.5 L) chicken or meat stock
  flavored with onion
1 chicken stock cube (optional)
salt
freshly-ground black pepper
1½ cups (2½ oz/75 g) dried melokhia leaves
2 Swiss chard (silverbeet) leaves
1 quantity Garlic Sauce (page 20)

For serving:
chopped onion
vinegar or lemon juice

Bring strained stock to a boil in a large saucepan and add crumbled stock cube if homemade chicken stock is used. Adjust seasoning with salt and pepper.

Measure melokhia leaves, then rub to crumble finely. Remove white stalks from chard and chop leaves finely.

Add melokhia and chard to boiling stock, return almost to a boil and simmer, uncovered, for 10 minutes. The melokhia swells and stays suspended in the stock.

Make Garlic Sauce following recipe on page 20, and add to soup. Cover pan and simmer for 2 minutes. Serve piping hot with a bowl of chopped onions soaked in vinegar or lemon juice to be added to individual taste.

NOTE: If a whole chicken has been simmered for stock, oven-roast the chicken with butter and serve at the same meal. Plain Boiled Rice (page 55) completes the meal.

# **Red lentil soup** Shourba ads

EGYPT

**Serves** 6
**Cooking time** 45 minutes

1½ cups (10 oz/300 g) dried red lentils
6 cups (48 fl oz/1.5 L) meat or chicken stock or
  water
1 yellow (brown) onion, grated
1 teaspoon ground cumin
salt
freshly-ground black pepper
1 tablespoon lemon juice

For serving:
1 quantity Onion Sauce (page 20)
olive oil
lemon wedges

Rinse lentils well in a sieve under cold running water.

Bring stock or water to a boil in a large soup pot or saucepan. Add lentils and onion and stir. Reduce heat to low, cover and simmer until lentils are tender, about 30 minutes. Do not stir during cooking. The lentils should have collapsed into a puree; for a finer texture, press through a sieve or puree in a blender.

Add cumin and salt and pepper to taste. If a thinner soup is desired, add water. Stir in lemon juice and heat gently.

Serve hot in deep soup bowls, topping each serving with Onion Sauce. Offer extra olive oil for drizzling and lemon wedges for squeezing into soup, according to individual taste, at the table. Serve with pita or other bread.

# Fava bean soup
## Ful nabed
EGYPT

**Serves** 6
**Cooking time** 1¾ hours

3 cups (18 oz/550 g) fava (broad) beans (see page 14)
cold water
1 teaspoon ground cumin
salt
freshly-ground black pepper
¼ cup (2 fl oz/60 ml) olive oil
1 tablespoon lemon juice

For serving:
finely-chopped fresh flat-leaf (Italian) parsley
lemon wedges

Cover beans well with cold water and let soak for 48 hours, skinned beans for 24 hours, changing water 2 or 3 times. Drain beans and remove skins if present (see page 14).

Place prepared beans in a large pot or saucepan with 6 cups (48 fl oz/1.5 L) water and bring to a slow simmer. Cover and simmer gently until very soft, about 1–1½ hours.

Puree cooked beans in a blender or press through a sieve using a wooden spoon, and return to pan. Add cumin, salt and pepper to taste, olive oil and lemon juice. Stir over gentle heat until bubbling.

Serve hot in deep bowls garnished with chopped parsley. Lemon juice is squeezed on according to individual taste. Flat bread or other bread should accompany this soup.

# Lentil and vermicelli soup
## Shourbat el ads
TUNISIA

**Serves** 6–8
**Cooking time** 45 minutes

1¾ cups (12 oz/350 g) red lentils
2 tablespoons olive oil
1 large onion, finely chopped
2 cloves garlic, crushed
1 teaspoon ground cumin
½ teaspoon ground coriander
8 cups (64 fl oz/2 L) chicken stock
salt and freshly-ground black pepper
2 tablespoons lemon juice
3½ oz (110 g) vermicelli pasta, broken into short lengths
2 tablespoons finely-chopped fresh flat-leaf (Italian) parsley

Place lentils in sieve and pick over to remove extra matter. Rinse under cold running water and drain.

Heat oil in a large saucepan. Add onion and cook until translucent, about 10 minutes. Add garlic, cumin and coriander, and cook gently for 1–2 minutes. Stir in lentils and stock, and bring to a boil. Reduce heat, cover and simmer gently until lentils are soft, about 30 minutes.

Add salt and pepper to taste, lemon juice and pasta. Return to a boil, stirring, and boil gently, uncovered, until pasta is tender, about 3–4 minutes. Stir in parsley and serve hot.

# Spicy soup with couscous
## Chorba hara bi keskou
ALGERIA

As this soup is made without meat stock, it is ideal for vegetarians. If you have traditional couscous, it will require longer cooking and should be added 15 minutes before end of cooking time.

**Serves** 6
**Cooking time** 45–50 minutes

4 tablespoons olive oil
1 small onion, finely chopped
2 cloves garlic, crushed
1 teaspoon Harissa (page 20)
1 tablespoon paprika
14-oz (425-g) can tomatoes, chopped but undrained
6 cups (48 fl oz/1.5 L) water
salt and freshly-ground black pepper
2 medium potatoes, about 12 oz (350 g) in total
½ cup (3 oz/90 g) instant couscous
3 tablespoons finely-chopped cilantro (fresh coriander) leaves

Heat oil in a large saucepan. Add onion and cook gently until transparent, about 10 minutes. Add garlic and cook for a few seconds. Add harissa to taste and cook gently, stirring, 1–2 minutes. Add paprika, tomatoes with their liquid, water, and salt and pepper to taste. Bring to a boil.

Peel potatoes, cut into ½-in (12-mm) cubes and add to soup. Cover pan and simmer until potatoes are tender, about 20 minutes. Stir in couscous and boil gently, uncovered, until couscous has swelled and softened, about 10 minutes, adding a little more water if necessary.

Adjust seasoning, adding more harissa if desired. Stir in cilantro, cover and let stand for 5 minutes. Serve hot in deep soup bowls with bread.

# Lamb soup with chickpeas and lentils Harira
## MOROCCO

Harira is the soup served each evening during Ramadan to break the fast and needs to be very nourishing. However, it is also served frequently throughout the year. Similar soups, with varying ingredients, are called "Chorba bil Lham" in Algeria, Tunisia and Libya.

**Serves** 6
**Cooking time** 1¾ hours

1 lb (500 g) boneless lamb shoulder
2 tablespoons ghee or olive oil
1 large onion, finely-chopped
½ teaspoon ground ginger
½ teaspoon freshly-ground black pepper
½ teaspoon ground cinnamon
1 teaspoon ground cumin
1 teaspoon ground turmeric
4 cups (32 fl oz/1 L) chicken stock
2 cups (16 fl oz/500 ml) water
½ cup (3 oz/90 g) brown lentils, rinsed
14-oz (425-g) can chickpeas, drained and rinsed
14-oz (425-g) can chopped tomatoes
3 tablespoons tomato paste
3 tablespoons chopped cilantro (fresh coriander)
3 tablespoons chopped fresh flat-leaf (Italian) parsley
salt
¾ cup (2 oz/60 g) crumbled vermicelli noodles (optional)

Trim lamb and cut into ½-in (12-mm) cubes. In a large soup pot or saucepan, heat ghee or olive oil, add onion and cook gently over low heat for 5 minutes. Stir in ginger, pepper, cinnamon, cumin and turmeric, and cook for a further 30 seconds. Increase heat to medium, add lamb and cook, stirring often, until lamb changes color. Stir in chicken stock, water, lentils, chickpeas, tomatoes and tomato paste. Cover and simmer until lamb and lentils are tender, about 1½ hours.

Stir in cilantro and parsley, and season to taste with salt. Bring soup to a boil and stir in vermicelli noodles if using. Continue to boil gently until noodles are tender, about 5 minutes. Serve soup in bowls with bread.

# Lamb and bread soup Fata

## EGYPT

**Serves** 6
**Cooking time** 2 hours

1½ lb (750 g) lean, boneless lamb
6 cups (48 fl oz/1.5 L) water
1 large onion, finely chopped
salt
freshly-ground black pepper
1 clove, or pinch ground mastic (optional)
½ cup (3½ oz/110 g) rice
1 cup (8 fl oz/250 ml) water, extra
2 tablespoons ghee or butter

To finish:
¼ cup (2 oz/60 g) ghee or butter
2–3 cloves garlic, crushed
¼ cup (2 fl oz/60 ml) red wine vinegar
2 rounds Egyptian Pita Bread (page 22) or other
   pita bread, toasted

Cut lamb into small cubes and place in a large pot or saucepan with cold water. Bring slowly to a boil, skimming when necessary.

Add onion and salt and pepper to taste, and stir. Add clove or ground mastic if using. (This overcomes the aroma of boiling lamb which some people dislike, but I find it unnecessary.) Cover and simmer gently until lamb is tender without falling apart, about 1½ hours.

While soup is cooking, wash rice and drain. Boil extra 1 cup (8 fl oz/250 ml) water in a separate pan, add 1 tablespoon ghee or butter, ½ teaspoon salt and rice, and return to a boil, stirring occasionally. Cover and simmer over low heat until tender, about 15 minutes.

Lift cooked meat from soup using a slotted spoon and drain. Heat remaining 1 tablespoon ghee or butter in a frying pan and fry lamb until browned all over. Remove from pan and keep hot.

Add ¼ cup (2 oz/60 g) ghee or butter to frying pan and heat. Add garlic and fry until lightly colored. Remove pan from heat, stir in vinegar then return to heat and boil for a few seconds. Remove pan from heat and set aside.

Place 1 round of toasted bread in a large tureen or casserole; cut into fourths, if desired. Spoon a little of garlic mixture over bread and top with half of cooked rice. Pour on some of soup then add another layer of bread and remaining rice. Put fried meat cubes on top and spoon on remaining garlic mixture. Add remaining soup and garnish with chopped parsley before serving.

NOTE: To simplify the preparation of this dish, the rice may be boiled in the soup after the meat cubes have been removed.

# Tomato, onion and preserved lemon salad Shalada bil matesha basila w'l'hamad m'rakhad

MOROCCO

Preserved lemons are essential for this salad and cannot be substituted. You can make your own (see page 16) or purchase them from a gourmet delicatessen or market.

**Serves** 6

2 lb (1 kg) firm ripe tomatoes, peeled and
   seeded
1 small red onion
½ **Preserved Lemon (page 16)**
⅓ **cup (3 fl oz/90 ml) olive oil**
1 tablespoon lemon juice
1 clove garlic, crushed
2 tablespoons chopped fresh flat-leaf (Italian)
   parsley
2 tablespoons chopped cilantro (fresh
   coriander) leaves
¼ teaspoon paprika
salt and freshly-ground black pepper

Cut tomatoes into small cubes. Slice onion as thinly as possible and separate into rings. Place tomatoes and onion rings in a bowl.

Discard pulp from preserved lemon and rinse peel well. Dry with paper towels, and cut crosswise into fine strips. Add to tomatoes and onion.

In a pitcher, mix olive oil, lemon juice, garlic, herbs, paprika, and salt and pepper to taste. Pour over salad, toss lightly, cover and let stand for 30 minutes. Serve at room temperature.

# Orange and olive salad
## Shalada bortokal wa'l'zaitun
MOROCCO, TUNISIA

**Serves** 6

**4 sweet oranges**
**1 red (Spanish) onion**
**¾ cup (3 oz/90 g) black olives, rinsed and**
**drained**
**¼ cup (2 fl oz/60 ml) olive oil**
**⅛ teaspoon cayenne pepper**
**1 teaspoon superfine (caster) sugar**
**¼ Preserved Lemon (page 16) (optional)**
**cilantro (fresh coriander) leaves for garnish**

Peel oranges using a serrated knife, removing all traces of white pith and outer membrane. Cut into ¼-in (5-mm) slices on plate to retain juices. Arrange orange slices on shallow serving platter. Slice onion thinly and separate slices into rings. Scatter onion rings and olives over orange slices.

Pour orange juice from plate into small bowl. Add olive oil, cayenne pepper and sugar, and beat well. Pour over salad.

Discard pulp from preserved lemon, rinse peel and cut into thin strips. Scatter over salad and garnish with cilantro leaves.

# Beet salad with oranges and walnuts
## Shalada baiba bil alchin wa'l gharghaa
ALGERIA

**Serves** 6

**6 medium beets (beetroots) with tops**
**salt**
**½ cup (2 oz/60 g) walnut pieces**
**2 sweet oranges**
**3 tablespoons olive oil**
**1 tablespoon red wine vinegar**
**freshly-ground black pepper**
**8–10 romaine (cos) lettuce leaves**

Cut tops from beets, leaving 1¼ in (3 cm) attached, and wash well. Place in a saucepan with water to cover and season with salt. Bring to a boil and cook until tender, 40–50 minutes. Drain and cover with cold water. When cool enough to handle, slip off skins. Cut beets in half and slice into wedges then place in a bowl.

Peel oranges with a serrated knife, removing all traces of white pith and outer membrane. Segment by cutting between visible membranes, catching juice in a bowl. Squeeze remains of oranges into juice bowl and reserve juice. Set orange segments aside separately.

Heat a dry frying pan over medium heat, add walnuts and toss until lightly toasted, 2–3 minutes. Transfer to a plate to cool then break into smaller pieces.

Combine juice in a bowl with vinegar, olive oil, and salt and pepper to taste. Beat with a fork then add half of dressing to beets. Toss lightly.

Tear lettuce leaves into pieces. Place in a large, shallow bowl and toss with remaining dressing. Top with beets and orange segments and sprinkle with walnuts. Serve immediately.

# Orange salad with carrot
## Shalada bortokal bil jazar
MOROCCO

**Moroccan orange salads are refreshing and palate-cleansing. They go well with meat and poultry dishes, although in Morocco salads are served as an appetizer and left on the table to be picked at during the remainder of the meal.**

**Serves** 6

**3 sweet oranges**
**2 medium carrots, shredded**
**orange juice**
**2 tablespoons lemon juice**
**3 teaspoons superfine (caster) sugar**
**2 tablespoons olive oil**
**salt and freshly-ground black pepper**
**cilantro (fresh coriander) leaves or fresh**
   **flat-leaf (Italian) parsley for garnish**
**1 tablespoon orange flower water**
**ground cinnamon for garnish**

Peel oranges using a serrated knife, removing all traces of white pith and outer membrane. Segment by cutting between visible membranes, catching juice in a bowl. Squeeze remains of oranges into bowl and reserve juice. Reserve one-fourth of orange segments and set aside. Place remaining segments in a bowl with carrot.

Make up 3 tablespoons orange juice using reserved juice and adding freshly-squeezed orange juice as needed. Combine orange juice, lemon juice and sugar in a small bowl, and stir until sugar is dissolved. Beat in oil and salt and pepper to taste. Pour over carrots and oranges and toss lightly. Cover and refrigerate to chill, along with reserved orange segments.

When ready to serve, transfer to shallow platter and garnish with reserved orange segments and cilantro leaves or parsley. Sprinkle with orange flower water and dust lightly with cinnamon.

VARIATION: ORANGE AND RADISH SALAD
Replace carrots with 15 medium-sized round, red radishes sliced very thinly. Toss together and place in shallow bowl lined with romaine (cos) lettuce leaves.

# Roasted tomato and pepper salad
## Salata mechouia
TUNISIA

Vegetables roasted on a fire are often cut up or pounded and mixed into a salad for serving as an appetizer. This version is excellent served with broiled (grilled) or barbecued meats, poultry or fish. If you do not like food to be too spicy, omit the chili peppers and add a pinch of cayenne pepper.

**Serves** 6

6 large, firm red tomatoes
2 green bell peppers (capsicums)
2 red bell peppers (capsicums)
2 fresh, hot red or green chili peppers
2 small yellow (brown) onions, whole and unpeeled
4 tablespoons olive oil
2 cloves garlic, crushed
salt and freshly-ground black pepper
1 tablespoon finely-chopped fresh flat-leaf (Italian) parsley
black olives for serving

Preheat oven to 425–450°F (220–230°C/Gas 7–8). Place tomatoes, bell peppers and onions on a baking sheet and bake for 15 minutes. Turn, add chili peppers and bake a further 15 minutes. Remove from oven, place bell peppers in a plastic bag, seal and let steam for 15 minutes. Peel tomatoes and cut into small pieces, draining juice and loose seeds. Cut chili peppers in half lengthwise, remove seeds and scrape flesh from skin. Peel and slice onions. When bell peppers are steamed, peel, cut in halves and remove seeds and membranes then cut into small squares.

In a bowl, beat chili pulp, oil and garlic. Add cooked vegetables and salt and pepper to taste, and mix lightly. Let cool to room temperature. Transfer to shallow serving dish and sprinkle with parsley. Arrange olives around edge or scatter on top.

## Saffron rice Roz bil za'fran
MOROCCO

**Serves** 4–5
**Cooking time** 20 minutes

2 cups (14 oz/440 g) medium-grain rice
2 tablespoons olive oil
3½ cups (28 fl oz/875 ml) water
½ teaspoon saffron threads
1 teaspoon salt

Put rice in a sieve and rinse under cold running water until water runs clear. Drain well.

Place a heavy-based saucepan over medium heat, add oil and rice, and stir for 1 minute to coat grains with oil. Add water, saffron threads and salt, and bring to a boil over high heat, stirring often. When boiling, reduce heat to low, cover tightly with lid and simmer until water is absorbed and holes appear in rice, about 15 minutes. Remove from heat and let stand, covered, for 10 minutes.

Fluff up with a fork and serve with tagines and seafood dishes, or as directed in recipes.

# Couscous Seksu
## NORTH AFRICA

North African nations serve steaming mounds of couscous with their flavorsome stews; in Egypt it is generally prepared as a dessert, and occasionally makes its appearance with stews.

Couscous is now readily available; for the curious, adventurous and patient, I have given directions for making your own. Allow plenty of time and give yourself lots of space. Once you have mastered the art, increase ingredients proportionately to make a larger quantity and store in an airtight container.

**Makes** about 2 cups (12 oz/375 g)

1 cup (6 oz/185 g) coarse semolina
¼–⅓ cup (2–3 fl oz/60–90 ml) cold water
¼–⅓ cup (1½–2 oz/45–60 g) all-purpose (plain) flour
¼ teaspoon salt

Place semolina in a large round baking dish or basin with flat base. Form into a circle leaving center clear.

Pour 2 tablespoons water in center, flick semolina into water with fingers, then work with palm of hand in a circular motion to moisten semolina evenly.

Mix flour with salt, and sprinkle half over semolina. Work into semolina, again using palm of hand and circular movements. Add a little more of water and flour so that small, round grains about the size of sesame seeds begin to form. The aim is to coat semolina grains with flour.

Turn out into a wide, medium-meshed wire sieve (a wooden framed sieve is ideal) set over a large cloth. Sieve and return grains from cloth to baking dish or basin, with any large lumps left on top of the grains in the sieve. The smaller grains in sieve are couscous—tip these into a bowl.

Work a little more flour and water into dish or basin contents to form more small ground grains. Sieve and sort again. Repeat until ingredients are formed into pellets of couscous, adding more flour and water as required. No more than ⅓ cup (2 oz/60 g) flour and ⅓ cup (3 fl oz/90 ml) water should be used to 1 cup (3 oz/90 g) semolina.

Line top section of a couscoussier or a colander with a piece of doubled muslin (cheesecloth) and put couscous in it, spreading it evenly.

Bring about 3 cups (24 fl oz/750 ml) water to a boil in bottom section of couscoussier or a deep saucepan, and place container with couscous on top. Container with couscous must not touch water. If using a colander, drape a kitchen towel around rim to ensure colander fits snugly, so steam does not escape. Cover with lid and steam for 10 minutes.

Turn out couscous onto a cloth and break up any lumps with fingers. Spread out and set aside for several hours in an airy place to dry thoroughly. Store in an airtight container, and use as directed in recipes.

# Boiled rice Roz

EGYPT

**Serves** 6
**Cooking time** 20 minutes

2 cups (14 oz/440 g) rice, long or short grain
water
salt
2 tablespoons ghee or butter

Place rice in a sieve and rinse under running water. Put into a bowl with 1 teaspoon salt and cover with cold water. Soak for 10 minutes, then drain in sieve. Do this well ahead of time required for cooking so that grains can dry. Spread it out in a dish if desired.

Heat ghee or butter in a heavy-based saucepan over medium heat. Add rice and stir until grains are well coated in fat, about 2 minutes. Add 3½ cups (28 fl oz/875 ml) water and 1 teaspoon salt, and bring to a boil, stirring occasionally. Reduce heat, cover pan tightly and cook over low heat for 15–20 minutes.

Remove pan from heat and let stand, covered, for 5–10 minutes. Fluff up rice with a fork and serve.

ALTERNATIVE COOKING METHOD: Drain rice after soaking; there is no need to let grains dry. Put 3½ cups (28 fl oz/375 ml) water, ghee or butter and salt into pan and bring to a boil. Add drained rice. Return to a boil, stirring once or twice, then reduce heat, cover and finish as above.

# Rice cooked in stock Ruzz mhammas

LIBYA

This recipe uses stock instead of water to cook the rice. Use a stock that complements the dish with which the rice is to be served: fish, meat or vegetarian stock can be used in place of chicken stock. Medium-grained rice can be substituted for long-grain.

**Serves** 6
**Cooking time** 25–30 minutes

2 cups (14 oz/440 g) rice, medium or long grain
2 tablespoons butter
1 small onion, finely chopped
3½ cups (28 fl oz/875 ml) chicken stock
salt and freshly-ground black pepper

Place rice in a sieve and rinse under running water. Drain well.

Melt butter in a large saucepan. Add onion and cook gently until translucent, about 10 minutes. Add rice and cook over low heat until opaque, stirring occasionally. Stir in stock and season with salt and pepper to taste. Increase heat and bring to a boil, stirring. Reduce heat, cover and simmer over low heat until water is absorbed and holes appear on surface of rice, about 15 minutes.

Remove pan from heat and let stand, covered, for 5 minutes. Fluff up rice with fork and transfer to warmed serving dish.

# Lentils, macaroni and rice in oil
# Koushari
EGYPT

This is classed as an "oil" dish by Coptic Egyptians and is prepared during periods of fasting when animal products cannot be taken. You may cook the lentils, macaroni and rice simultaneously in three pots, or if, like me, you like to keep pots to a minimum, use the method given. This is the way they prepare it in Egypt anyway.

**Serves** 6
**Cooking time** 1½–1¾ hours

1 cup (7 oz/220 g) brown lentils
water
salt
1 cup (5 oz/150 g) small macaroni pasta
1 cup (7 oz/220 g) short-grain rice
2 tablespoons olive oil
Onion Sauce (page 20)
1 cup (8 fl oz/250 ml) tomato puree

Place lentils in a sieve and wash well under running water. Place in a large pot or saucepan with 3 cups (24 fl oz/750 ml) water and 1 teaspoon salt. Bring to a boil, then simmer until tender but still intact, about 40 minutes. Drain and set aside.

Clean same pot or pan, and add 4 cups (32 fl oz/1 L) water. Bring to a boil, add 2 teaspoons salt and macaroni. Stir until water returns to a boil then cook, uncovered and stirring occasionally, until tender, 15 minutes. Drain and set aside.

Clean pot or pan again and dry. Rinse rice well in a sieve under running water and drain. Heat oil in pot or pan over medium heat, add rice and cook, stirring, for 2–3 minutes. Add 2 cups (16 fl oz/500 ml) water and 1 teaspoon salt, and bring to a boil, stirring occasionally. Cover and simmer over low heat until rice is tender, about 15 minutes. Remove pan from heat and let stand, covered, for 5 minutes so that grains separate.

Make Onion Sauce following directions on page 20. Add tomato puree and bring to a boil.

Add lentils and macaroni to cooked rice and toss together lightly with a fork. Pour hot Onion Sauce and tomato on top, toss again and cover with lid. Cook over low heat for 10 minutes. Serve hot with salads, grilled fish or shrimp (prawns).

# Couscous with lamb and vegetables
## Seksu bil lham
MOROCCO

Couscous, as served in Morocco (and Algeria and Tunisia), is presented at the end of a banquet to ensure guests do not depart hungry; in the home, it is a popular Friday lunch, using leftover meat pieces and bones, and vegetables. Usually the meat content is just enough to add extra flavor to the copious broth, but if required for a main course, the amount of meat can be increased. Lamb, chicken and fish are usually prepared for couscous, with beef seldom used, but it can substitute in this recipe. Moroccans often add saffron, but as its delicate flavor can be masked by other ingredients, it can be omitted; harissa is a "must" in Tunisia, although it is also used in Morocco.

**Serves** 6
**Cooking time** 1¾ hours

2 lb (1 kg) boneless lamb leg meat, cubed
2 tablespoons olive oil
3 medium onions, cut into quarters
2 cloves garlic, crushed
3-in (7.5-cm) cinnamon stick
½ teaspoon ground turmeric
3 tablespoons chopped fresh flat-leaf (Italian) parsley
3 tablespoons chopped cilantro (fresh coriander) leaves
1 lb (500 g) ripe tomatoes, peeled and chopped
2 tablespoons tomato paste
3 cups (24 fl oz/750 ml) water
salt and freshly-ground black pepper
4 medium carrots, peeled and cut into quarters lengthwise
4 small white turnips, peeled and cut into quarters
14 oz (425 g) can chickpeas, drained
1 quantity Basic Couscous (page 19)
1 cup (4 oz/125 g) shelled fresh or frozen fava (broad) beans (optional)
1 lb (500 g) zucchini (courgettes), trimmed and cut into quarters lengthwise
½ quantity Harissa (page 20) for serving (optional)

Trim excess fat from lamb. Warm oil in a large saucepan. Add onions, garlic, cinnamon and turmeric and cook gently for 5 minutes. Increase heat, add lamb and cook, stirring often, until lamb is sealed, about 5 minutes. Add herbs, tomatoes, tomato paste, water, and salt and pepper to taste. Reduce heat, cover and simmer for 45 minutes. Add carrots, turnips and chickpeas, cover and simmer for 30 minutes.

Soak couscous as directed in recipe on page 19, separating grains with a fork.

Add fava beans if using and zucchini to saucepan, increase heat and bring to a boil. Place couscous in prepared steamer and place on top of saucepan, sealing edges of steamer with aluminum foil as described on page 19. Cook, uncovered, for 20 minutes, stirring couscous occasionally with fork.

Turn out couscous onto a heated platter, and pour over melted butter. Toss lightly then mound into peak. Garnish with some lamb and vegetables, if desired. Place remaining lamb and vegetables, discarding cinnamon, into a deep serving dish, adding broth from pan. If serving with harissa, place harissa in a small bowl and mix with ¾ cup (6 fl oz/180 ml) broth.

# Bedouin chicken and vegetable couscous Seksu bidaoui

## MOROCCO, TUNISIA, ALGERIA

**Serves** 6
**Cooking time** 1¼ hours

1 chicken, about 3 lb (1.5 kg)
3 tablespoons ghee or butter
1 onion, finely chopped
2 cloves garlic, crushed
1 teaspoon paprika
½ teaspoon ground ginger
½ teaspoon ground cinnamon
2 tablespoons chopped cilantro (fresh
   coriander)
2 tablespoons chopped fresh flat-leaf (Italian)
   parsley
3 cups (24 fl oz/750 ml) water
4 tomatoes, peeled, seeded and chopped
salt and freshly-ground black pepper
4 carrots, peeled and cut into quarters
   lengthwise
4 zucchini (courgettes), cut into quarters
   lengthwise
12 oz (375 g) butternut pumpkin (squash),
   peeled, seeded and cubed
1½ cups (7 oz/220 g) shelled green peas
14-oz (425-g) can chickpeas, drained and rinsed
2½ cups (1 lb/500 g) Basic Couscous (page 19)
3 teaspoons Harissa (page 20) for serving

Joint chicken into 8 pieces. Heat ghee or butter in a large saucepan or base of a couscoussier, add chicken and cook over high heat until browned on each side. Reduce heat to low, add onion and cook gently for 5 minutes. Stir in garlic, paprika, ginger and cinnamon, and cook, stirring occasionally, for 1 minute. Stir in herbs, water and tomatoes, and season with salt and pepper to taste. Bring to a gentle boil, cover and simmer over low heat for 25 minutes. Stir in carrot, cutting pieces in half if too long, and simmer for a further 15 minutes. Stir in butternut squash and cook for 5 minutes. Stir in zucchini, green peas and chickpeas, and cook until chicken and vegetables are tender, a further 15 minutes.

While chicken stew is cooking, prepare and steam couscous as directed on page 19, either over stew or a saucepan of boiling water.

To serve, pile couscous on a large, warm platter, make a well in center and pile chicken and vegetables on top, letting some tumble down sides. Moisten with a little broth from stew. Put remaining broth into a bowl, stir in harissa and place a ladle in bowl. The harissa-flavored broth is placed at the table and then added to couscous as required by each diner.

# Tuna with charmoula
## Thon bi' chermoula
MOROCCO

The herb and spice marinade, charmoula, given in this recipe can be used for lamb, poultry and other seafood, which is then broiled, grilled, barbecued, panfried or baked. This is just one version of many in the Moroccan kitchen—swordfish may also be prepared in this manner. The preserved lemon may be omitted if not available, but it is recommended.

**Serves** 4–6
**Cooking time** 4–6 minutes

4–6 tuna steaks, about 4 oz (125 g) each
¼ Preserved Lemon (page 16), julienned, or
   fresh lemon slices for garnish

For charmoula:
¼ Preserved Lemon (page 16)
2 cloves garlic
3 tablespoons chopped cilantro (fresh
   coriander) leaves
3 tablespoons chopped fresh flat-leaf (Italian)
   parsley
⅛ teaspoon powdered saffron (optional)
½ teaspoon paprika
⅛–¼ teaspoon cayenne pepper
½ teaspoon ground cumin
½ teaspoon salt
2 tablespoons lemon juice
4 tablespoons olive oil

Remove skin from tuna if present. Rinse tuna, pat dry with paper towels, and place in a glass or ceramic dish.

To make charmoula: Discard pulp from preserved lemon, rinse peel and pat dry. Place with remaining ingredients in a food processor and process to a coarse puree.

Pour charmoula over tuna, reserving about 6 tablespoons for serving. Turn tuna in marinade to coat, cover and refrigerate for at least 2 hours or overnight.

Drain tuna, leaving thin coating of charmoula, and reserve remaining marinade. Cook tuna under preheated hot broiler (grill) or on barbecue until just cooked, about 4–6 minutes, turning carefully and brushing with marinade during cooking.

Serve hot with 1 teaspoon reserved charmoula on each serving and garnished with preserved lemon or lemon slices.

VARIATION: TUNA KEBABS
Use steaks cut 1 in (2.5 cm) thick, remove skin and cut into cubes. Marinate in charmoula as above, thread onto skewers, and broil (grill) or cook on barbecue, turning and basting often with reserved charmoula.

# Fish with rice Sayyadiah

## EGYPT

**Serves** 4
**Cooking time** 1 hour

4 whole fish, about 12 oz (375 g) each
juice of 1 lemon
salt
freshly-ground black pepper
3 cloves garlic, finely chopped or crushed
1 teaspoon ground cumin
2 tablespoons oil
2 medium-sized onions, finely chopped
2 cups (14 oz/440 g) long-grain rice
3½ cups (28 fl oz/875 ml) hot water
all-purpose (plain) flour
oil for shallow-frying
lemon wedges and fresh flat-leaf (Italian)
  parsley sprigs for garnish

Scale and gut fish, leaving heads on. Rinse and wipe dry with paper towels. Rub surfaces and cavities with lemon juice and season with salt and pepper. Cover and set aside for 30–45 minutes.

In a small bowl, mix garlic with cumin.

Heat oil in a deep saucepan, add onions and gently fry until very soft and golden, 15–20 minutes. Rinse rice, drain well and add to onions. Stir over medium heat for 2–3 minutes, then stir in hot water. Bring to a boil, reduce heat to low, cover pan and cook gently for 20 minutes.

Make 3–4 deep slits on each side of fish and fill slits with garlic-cumin mixture. Coat fish with flour and shallow-fry in hot oil until golden-brown and cooked through. Transfer to a dish and keep hot.

Add about 2 tablespoons of oil in which fish was fried to cooked rice, and stir through using a fork. Cover pan and let stand for 5 minutes.

To serve, pile rice on a platter, arrange fish on top and garnish with lemon wedges and parsley sprigs.

# Little tuna turnovers Thon ajin

## LIBYA

**Makes** about 36

**For pie crust:**
**2 cups (10 oz/300 g) all-purpose (plain) flour**
**½ teaspoon salt**
**¾ cup (6 fl oz/180 ml) warm water**
**⅓ cup (3 fl oz/90 ml) olive oil**
**1 egg, beaten**
**oil, for shallow-frying**

**For tuna filling:**
**1 tablespoon olive oil**
**1 medium onion, finely chopped**
**2 hard-cooked (boiled) eggs**
**6–7 oz (185–220 g) canned tuna chunks**
**in brine**
**1–2 tablespoons lemon juice**
**2 tablespoons chopped fresh flat-leaf (Italian)**
**parsley**
**salt and freshly-ground black pepper**

To make pie crust: Sift flour and salt into a bowl and make a well in center. Place water, oil and egg in a separate bowl and beat well. Pour egg mixture into flour. Using wooden spoon, mix thoroughly to form a soft dough. Gradually stir in egg until dough is smooth. Turn out onto a lightly-floured work surface, dust top with flour and knead until no longer sticky, adding more flour if necessary. Divide dough into 2 balls, cover with folded kitchen towel, and let stand for 30 minutes.

To make tuna filling: Heat oil in a small frying pan. Add onion and cook gently until translucent, 6–8 minutes. Transfer cooked onion to a bowl. Remove shells from eggs, mash eggs and add to onion with 1 tablespoon lemon juice, drained tuna, parsley, and salt and pepper to taste. Stir well to break up tuna, taste and add more lemon juice if necessary.

To make turnovers: Knead 1 dough ball on a floured surface, about 5–6 turns. Roll out until fairly thin. Cut into 3½-in (9-cm) rounds with floured cutter, twisting cutter to separate each round from rest of pie crust. Lift off trimmings and place under kitchen towel. Brush edge of each round with water and place 1 heaping teaspoon tuna filling in center. Fold over and press edges together to seal. Press edges with tines of fork, or use thimble or tip of coffee spoon, to make scalloped edges. Place on a cloth-lined tray. Repeat with remaining ball of dough, including pie crust trimmings, and filling.

To cook, add oil for shallow-frying to a depth of ¾ in (2 cm) in a large frying pan. Heat well, until scrap of dough placed in oil sizzles immediately. Add turnovers, working in batches of 5–7 at a time, and cook until golden-brown, about 3 minutes, turning to brown evenly. Remove using a slotted spoon and drain on paper towels. Serve hot.

# Fried pastries with anchovies and egg Brik bil anchouwa
## TUNISIA

In Tunisia, brik are made with a special pastry called malsouqa, more widely known as the warka or ouarka of Moroccan cuisine. Whereas filo can be used as a substitute in dishes such as oven-baked bisteeya, spring roll wrappers, made with wheat flour and prepared in a similar way to the North African pastry leaves, are a better substitute for this recipe. The skins fry crisply and stay crisp, unlike filo which softens quickly with moist filling. Do not assemble all briks at once or the filling will soak through the skins, tearing them.

**Makes** 4

**four 8-in (20-cm) square spring roll wrappers**
**1 tablespoon olive oil**
**1 large onion, finely chopped**
**1½ tablespoons finely-chopped, drained canned anchovy fillets**
**2 tablespoons chopped fresh flat-leaf (Italian) parsley**
**3 teaspoons capers, drained, and chopped if large**
**freshly-ground black pepper**
**olive or other oil for shallow-frying**
**1 egg white, lightly beaten**
**4 small fresh eggs (each about 1½ oz/45 g)**

Separate spring roll wrappers and seal remainder. Stack wrappers on a cutting board, cover with a folded clean kitchen towel and set aside.

Heat olive oil in a small frying pan. Add onion and cook gently until very soft and translucent, about 12–15 minutes, stirring often. Add anchovies and mash in.

Remove pan from heat, stir in parsley, capers and pepper to taste, and let cool. Divide into 4 portions in pan.

Add oil for shallow-frying to a depth of ¼ in (5 mm) in a 10-in (25-cm) frying pan and heat well over medium heat.

Place 1 wrapper on a plate and brush around edge with beaten egg white. Place 1 portion onion filling in a heap on one side, with edge of filling just touching center. Make indent in filling with soup spoon and break 1 egg into it. Fold wrapper over to enclose filling and press edges to seal.

Slide brik immediately into hot oil and shallow-fry until golden-brown and crisp, about 45 seconds on each side, turning brik over using two spatulas. Lift out and drain on paper towels. Repeat to make and cook remaining briks. Serve immediately while hot.

VARIATIONS: Other fillings may be used in place of anchovies, such as 3 oz (90 g) canned tuna in oil, drained and flaked; or 3 tablespoons chopped, cooked chicken, omitting capers if using chicken.

# Fish tagine with charmoula and tomato Hout chtetha

ALGERIA

**Serves** 4
**Cooking time** 25–30 minutes

1 quantity Charmoula (page 19)
4 firm white fish cutlets (steaks) or thick fillets,
    such as snapper, blue-eye cod or sea bass,
    about 7 oz (220 g) each
1½ lb (750 g) tomatoes, peeled, seeded and
    chopped
2 tablespoons tomato paste
½ teaspoon sugar
1 clove garlic, crushed
1 tablespoon lemon juice
2 tablespoons olive oil
½ teaspoon cumin
1 teaspoon paprika
¼ teaspoon cayenne pepper
2 tablespoons finely-chopped fresh flat-leaf
    (Italian) parsley
salt and freshly-ground black pepper
3–4 bay leaves, preferably fresh

Make charmoula according to directions on page 19, omitting preserved lemon from that recipe.

Place fish in a shallow nonmetallic dish, add charmoula and rub into each side of fish. Cover and set aside for 20 minutes.

In a saucepan, mix tomatoes with tomato paste, sugar, lemon juice, garlic, olive oil, cumin, paprika, cayenne pepper, parsley, and salt and pepper to taste. Bring to a boil, cover and simmer for 15 minutes, mashing tomatoes to a rough puree with a fork. Remove pan from heat and set aside to cool until just warm.

Preheat oven to 400°F (200°C/Gas 6).

Lightly oil a baking dish large enough to take fish in a single layer. Place bay leaves on base and arrange fish cutlets on top, pouring marinade over them. Spread tomato mixture over fish, cover with lid or aluminum foil, and bake for 15 minutes.

Remove from oven, uncover and bake until fish flakes when tested and sauce is thick, a further 10–15 minutes. Serve hot from baking dish.

# Spiced shrimp Kruvit m'hammar
## MOROCCO

**Serves** 4
**Cooking time** 5–6 minutes

1½ lb (750 g) raw medium shrimp (prawns)
salt
⅓ cup (3 fl oz/90 ml) olive oil
1 teaspoon ground cumin
1 teaspoon ground ginger
1 tablespoon chopped fresh red chili
4 garlic cloves, finely chopped
1 teaspoon ground turmeric
1½ teaspoons paprika
¼ cup (2 fl oz/60 ml) water
3 tablespoons finely-chopped cilantro (fresh
   coriander)
lemon wedges for serving
crusty bread for serving

Peel and devein shrimp, leaving tails intact. Place in a colander and rinse under cold running water. Drain then shake well to remove excess water. Sprinkle with about 1 teaspoon salt, toss through and set aside.

Heat a large frying pan over medium heat, and when hot, add oil. Stir in cumin, ginger, garlic, turmeric and paprika. Cook until fragrant, add chili and cook, stirring, for 30 seconds, then add prawns. Increase heat slightly and cook prawns, tossing frequently, until they are firm and turn pink, 4–5 minutes. Stir in cilantro and ½ cup (4 fl oz/125 ml) water, bring to a simmer and remove from heat. Serve immediately with lemon wedges and crusty bread.

## Roast stuffed chicken
# Farroog mahshi
EGYPT

**Serves** 6
**Cooking time** 2 hours

2 chickens, about 2 lb (1 kg) each
salt
freshly-ground black pepper
¼ cup (2 oz/60 g) butter, melted

**For stuffing:**
1 cup (6 oz/185 g) coarse bulgur (burghul)
water
livers and hearts from chickens
1 large onion, finely chopped
2 tablespoons butter
2 tablespoons finely-chopped fresh flat-leaf
   (Italian) parsley
1 teaspoon dried mint
salt
freshly-ground black pepper
1 cup (8 fl oz/250 ml) chicken stock made from
   remaining giblets or stock cube

Wipe chickens with paper towels, season inside and out with salt and pepper, and cover and refrigerate until required.

Place bulgur in a bowl with enough water to cover and let soak for 5 minutes. Drain in a sieve, pressing with back of a spoon to extract all moisture.

Clean and finely chop livers and hearts. If chickens are without giblets, use 4 oz (125 g) chicken livers. Heat butter in a frying pan and gently fry onion until translucent. Add chopped liver and heart, and fry just long enough for color to change. Remove pan from heat. Stir in bulgur, parsley, mint rubbed to a powder, and salt and pepper to taste. Add stock, cover and cook over low heat for 5 minutes. Remove from heat and let cool.

Preheat oven to 350°F (180°C/Gas 4). Pack chicken cavity loosely with stuffing, close opening with poultry skewers and tie legs together with string. Put melted butter in a baking dish, add chickens breast-side up and baste with melted butter. Bake for 1½ hours, turning chickens on their sides during cooking then breast-side up for the final 10 minutes to complete browning.

Remove chickens to a plate and spoon stuffing onto serving platter. Joint chickens and place on top of stuffing. Keep hot.

Add a little hot water to browned juices in baking dish and bring to a boil, stirring to dissolve. Strain sauce over chicken and serve.

# Chicken stuffed with couscous, almonds and raisins
## Djej mahshe bil seksu
MOROCCO

When Moroccan cuisine was developing, a whole chicken was usually steamed over boiling water, as domestic ovens were unknown. Oven-cooking is now becoming more common, and it does improve the flavor of this delicious dish. The following method is a combination of roasting and steaming, which gives succulent, moist chicken full of flavor. Normally the stuffing makes use of leftover couscous from a previous meal; if you do have leftover couscous, use 1¼ cups (8 oz/250 g) cooked couscous, omitting the boiling water-salt-butter mixture used in the stuffing ingredients.

**Serves** 4
**Cooking time** 2¼ hours

3½ lb (1.75 kg) roasting chicken
salt and freshly-ground black pepper
paprika
1 cup (8 fl oz/250 ml) water
2 tablespoons butter, softened

For couscous stuffing:
⅓ cup (1½ oz/45 g) raisins
½ cup (4 fl oz/125 ml) water
½ teaspoon salt
¼ cup (2 oz/60 g) butter
½ cup (3 oz/90 g) couscous
½ cup (2½ oz/75 g) whole blanched almonds
½ teaspoon sugar
½ teaspoon ground cinnamon
¼ teaspoon paprika
freshly-ground black pepper

Clean chicken cavity if necessary, rinse and dry with paper towels then season cavity with salt and pepper.

To make couscous stuffing: Place raisins in a small heatproof bowl and add enough boiling water to barely cover. Let stand until plump, about 10 minutes. Combine ½ cup (4 fl oz/125 ml) water, half of butter and salt to taste in a saucepan, bring to a boil then remove from heat. Stir in couscous, cover and let stand, until water is absorbed, about 10 minutes.

Melt remaining butter in a frying pan, add almonds and cook until golden-brown, about 2 minutes. Add almonds and butter, sugar, cinnamon, paprika, pepper to taste, and drained raisins to couscous. Mix thoroughly and lightly with a fork.

Preheat oven to 350–375°F (180–190°C/Gas 4–5). Pack chicken cavity loosely with stuffing, close opening with poultry skewers and tie legs together with string. Tuck wing tips under body and secure neck skin with a poultry skewer. Season with salt, pepper and paprika. Place breast-side up in a baking pan and pour in water. Spread softened butter over chicken and bake until cooked, basting often, about 2 hours. To test if chicken is cooked, push a leg toward the breast; chicken is cooked when leg moves easily.

Transfer chicken to a warm platter, cover with aluminum foil and let rest in a warm place for 10 minutes. Pour pan juices over chicken, if desired. Serve with couscous stuffing.

# Chicken with preserved lemon and olives Djej makalli

## MOROCCO

This would have to be one of the best-known Moroccan recipes. Usually a whole chicken is jointed, but boneless, skinless chicken breasts are recommended in this recipe. Chicken livers are often added to give body to the sauce—the following recipe uses much less liquid than usual, so they are excluded. If you do not have preserved lemons, you can use the grated rind of 1 lemon in cooking, and finish with blanched julienne strips of lemon rind—not the same, although the dish still tastes good. While this dish is often served on its own as a separate course in Morocco, it is excellent served with rice (see page 55).

**Serves** 6
**Cooking time** 35 minutes

3 cloves garlic, crushed
½ teaspoon ground ginger
½ teaspoon ground cumin
¼ teaspoon freshly-ground black pepper
⅛ teaspoon cayenne pepper
½ teaspoon ground turmeric
pinch of powdered saffron (optional)
2 tablespoons olive oil
6 single (half) chicken breast fillets
1 large onion, finely chopped
¾ cup (6 fl oz/180 ml) chicken stock
3 tablespoons chopped cilantro (fresh
    coriander) leaves
3 tablespoons chopped fresh flat-leaf (Italian)
    parsley
salt
1 Preserved Lemon (page 16)
18 kalamata olives
1–2 tablespoons lemon juice

Combine garlic, spices and 1 teaspoon oil in a large dish. Add chicken, rub with spice paste, cover and refrigerate for 2–3 hours or overnight.

Heat remaining oil in a large frying pan with lid to fit. Add onion and cook gently until translucent, about 10 minutes. Increase heat, add chicken and cook, turning, until chicken becomes white, about 5 minutes.

Add stock to marinating dish and stir well to mix with any remaining marinade. Add stock mixture to chicken with herbs and salt to taste. Reduce heat to low, cover and simmer gently for 10 minutes.

Meanwhile, remove pulp from preserved lemon and discard. Rinse peel and cut into julienne strips. Place olives in a small saucepan and add enough water to cover. Bring to a boil then drain. Repeat twice until there is no trace of bitterness.

Add preserved lemon peel strips and olives to chicken, cover and simmer for a further 10 minutes. Add lemon juice and seasoning to taste. Serve hot.

# Chicken and almond pie Bisteeya
## MOROCCO

Bisteeya is traditionally made with pigeon (chicken is a popular substitute) and warkha, a special paper-thin pastry (filo is an alternative). While it is fried in Morocco, it is easier to bake if using filo.

**Serves** 6
**Cooking time** 1¾ hours

⅓ cup (3 oz/90 g) butter
1 large onion, grated
2 cloves garlic, finely chopped
1 teaspoon ground ginger
¼ teaspoon ground turmeric
¼ teaspoon cayenne pepper
pinch of saffron powder (optional)
3-in (7.5-cm) cinnamon stick
3 lb (1.5 kg) chicken, quartered
2 tablespoons chopped fresh flat-leaf (Italian) parsley
2 tablespoons chopped cilantro (fresh coriander) leaves
salt
2 cups (16 fl oz/500 ml) hot water
3 tablespoons lemon juice
6 egg yolks
¾ cup (3 oz/90 g) whole blanched almonds, chopped
1½ teaspoons ground cinnamon
¼ cup (1 oz/30 g) confectioners' (icing) sugar, sifted
½ cup (4 fl oz/125 ml) melted butter
12 sheets filo (phyllo) pastry
confectioners' (icing) sugar for garnish
ground cinnamon (optional) for garnish

Melt ¼ cup (2 fl oz/60 g) butter in a large saucepan. Add onion, garlic and spices, and stir gently over low heat for 5 minutes. Increase heat to medium, add chicken and cook, turning occasionally, until no longer pink, about 10 minutes. Add chopped herbs, 1 teaspoon salt and hot water. Cover and simmer over low heat until tender, about 1 hour. Remove pan from heat and let stand for 30 minutes. Remove chicken using a slotted spoon and discard cinnamon stick. Return pan to heat and boil liquid rapidly until reduced to about 1½ cups (12 fl oz/375 ml). Shred chicken meat into thick strips about 1½ in (4 cm) long, discarding skin and bones; set aside.

Stir lemon juice into reduced liquid and add more salt if required. Reduce heat. Whisk egg yolks in a heatproof bowl. Whisk in half of reduced liquid, then pour back into pan. Using a wooden spoon, stir over low heat until sauce is thick and coats back of spoon, 2–3 minutes. Stir in chicken meat and remove pan from heat. Preheat oven to 325–350°F (170–180°C/Gas 3–4).

Melt remaining butter in a small frying pan and fry almonds until lightly browned, about 2 minutes. Transfer to a bowl, stir in cinnamon and sugar, and set aside.

Brush a 12–14-in (30–35-cm) metal pizza pan with melted butter. Stack 6 sheets filo pastry on a cutting board, keeping remainder covered. Brush top sheet with butter and place on pizza pan with two ends overhanging. Brush next sheet and place at an angle to first sheet. Repeat with remaining sheets, fanning so there is an even overhang of pastry around pan.

Spread chicken filling evenly in pan, patting flat with spatula. Top with 1 filo sheet, folded so it covers chicken. Brush with butter and sprinkle almond mixture evenly over top. Bring overhanging pastry over top all around, and brush with butter. Stack remaining 5 sheets filo, brush with butter and place on pie in same way as

base, leaving top sheet unbuttered. Trim overhanging filo with scissors to even edge. Using rubber spatula to lift edge of pie, tuck overhanging filo underneath.

Brush top with butter and bake until golden-brown, about 40 minutes. Remove and sift confectioners' sugar on top immediately. Lift onto serving platter. If desired, sprinkle lines of cinnamon to make a lattice pattern on top. Serve hot.

# Chicken with apricots and honey
## Djej wa'l mashmash bil 'assel
MOROCCO

**Serves** 4
**Cooking time** 1 hour

1 chicken, about 3½ lb (1.75 kg)
2 tablespoons ghee or butter
1 onion, finely chopped
1 teaspoon ground cinnamon
1 teaspoon ground ginger
⅛ teaspoon cayenne pepper
⅛ teaspoon powdered saffron
1 tablespoon chopped cilantro (fresh coriander)
1½ cups (12 fl oz/375 ml) chicken stock
salt and freshly-ground black pepper
1 lb (500 g) fresh apricots
3 tablespoons honey
2 tablespoons toasted sesame seeds

Joint chicken into 8 pieces. Heat ghee or butter in a saucepan, add chicken pieces and cook, turning, until browned on each side. Reduce heat to low, add onion and cook gently for 5 minutes. Add cinnamon, ginger and cayenne pepper, and cook over low heat for 1 minute, stirring often. Add saffron, cilantro and chicken stock, and season to taste with salt and pepper. Cover and simmer over low heat until chicken is tender, 45–50 minutes.

Wash apricots, cut in halves and remove stones. Place apricot halves, cut-side up, around chicken and drizzle with honey. Cover and simmer until apricots are hot, about 5 minutes. Serve, sprinkling each portion with toasted sesame seeds.

NOTE: When fresh apricots are out of season, use 14-oz (425-g) can apricot halves in natural juice, drained. As a variation, 1⅓ cups (8 oz /250 g) pitted prunes can be used in place of the apricots; add to chicken for final 10 minutes of cooking.

# Grilled spiced chicken Djej mechoui

## MOROCCO

**Serves** 4
**Cooking time** 30–35 minutes

2 chickens, about 1½ lb (750 g) each
2 garlic cloves, crushed
1 teaspoon salt
1 teaspoon paprika
¼ teaspoon cayenne pepper
1 teaspoon ground cumin
½ teaspoon ground coriander
½ teaspoon freshly-ground black pepper
1 tablespoon lemon juice
1 tablespoon olive oil
1 tablespoon cilantro (fresh coriander) leaves
  for serving
2 lemons, cut into wedges, for serving

Cut chickens in half, removing backbone and cutting through breast. Push a long bamboo skewer through each half from tip of breast and through thigh and leg, to keep chickens in shape during cooking.

In a bowl, mix garlic, salt, paprika, cayenne pepper, cumin, coriander and black pepper. Stir in lemon juice and oil. Rub spice mixture all over chicken halves, place in a dish, cover and marinate in refrigerator for 1 hour.

Prepare a charcoal fire or preheat barbecue. Place chickens on grill plate, skin-side up, and cook over medium heat until browned on each side. Remove from grill plate and wrap each half in aluminum foil. Return wrapped chicken to grill plate and cook for a further 20 minutes, turning packages with tongs occasionally. When cooked, remove chicken from foil and cook until browned, a further 3 minutes each side, brushing with any marinade from dish. Scatter with cilantro leaves and serve with lemon wedges.

# meat

## Lamb tagine with dates
## Tagine lham bil beleh
MOROCCO

**Fresh dates feature in this dish; the dried dates are added to extend the flavor and thicken the sauce. You can serve it with Basic Couscous (page 19); although in Morocco, a tagine is served on its own.**

**Serves** 6
**Cooking time** 1¾ hours

2 lb (1 kg) boneless lamb leg or shoulder meat
2 tablespoons butter
1 large white onion, finely chopped
1½ cups (12 fl oz/375 ml) water
1 teaspoon ground ginger
1 teaspoon ground cinnamon
⅓ cup (2 oz/60 g) chopped dried pitted dates
salt and freshly-ground black pepper
2 tablespoons honey
2 tablespoons lime juice
12 fresh dates
1 tablespoon butter, extra
¼ cup (1 oz/30 g) whole blanched almonds
fresh lime slices or strips of Preserved Lemon
   peel (page 16) for garnish

Trim excess fat from lamb and cut into 1-in (2.5-cm) cubes. Melt butter in a large, heavy-based saucepan. Add onion and cook gently until translucent, about 10 minutes. Increase heat, add lamb and cook until sealed, stirring often. Stir in water, spices and chopped dried dates, and season with salt and pepper to taste. Cover and simmer over low heat until lamb is tender, about 1½ hours. Stir in honey and lime juice and adjust seasoning if required. Place whole fresh dates on top, cover and simmer for 5 minutes.

Melt extra butter in a small frying pan. Add almonds and cook until golden. Remove to a plate.

To serve, transfer lamb tagine to a serving dish and arrange fresh dates on top. Sprinkle with almonds and garnish with lime slices or strips of preserved lemon peel.

# Lamb and okra casserole Bamia

## EGYPT

**Serves** 5–6
**Cooking time** 2–2½ hours

2 lb (1 kg) boneless stewing lamb or beef
2 tablespoons ghee or butter
1 large onion, finely chopped
½ teaspoon ground cumin
14-oz (425-g) can tomatoes, chopped
2 tablespoons tomato paste
½ cup (4 fl oz/125 ml) stock or water
½ teaspoon sugar
salt and freshly-ground black pepper
1 lb (500 g) fresh okra
1 tablespoon ghee
Garlic Sauce (page 20)
Boiled Rice (page 55) for serving

Trim meat and cut into 1-in (2.5-cm) cubes. Heat ghee or butter in a heavy-based pan and brown meat on all sides, adding a single layer of meat to pan at a time. Transfer to a baking dish (casserole) with tight-fitting lid.

Reduce heat, add onion to pan and fry gently until translucent. Add cumin, tomatoes, tomato paste and stock, and stir well to lift browned juices.

Pour over lamb in dish, add sugar, and salt and pepper to taste. Cover and bake for 1½ hours.

Trim okra stem tips but do not cut into pod. Leave top part of cone intact. Rinse, drain and dry. Heat ghee in a pan, add okra and fry over medium heat for 3 minutes, tossing gently.

Arrange okra on top of meat in baking dish, cover and cook until meat is tender, a further 40 minutes.

Prepare Garlic Sauce following directions on page 20 and pour over bamia while hot. Serve at the table from baking dish, with rice in a separate dish.

# Lamb and quince stew
## Maraqat al-safarjal
TUNISIA

In North Africa, quinces are a popular addition to meat stews, where their refreshing tartness and fragrance is appreciated. Their use goes back to Persian influence in these regions.

**Serves** 6
**Cooking time** 1¾ hours

2 lb (1 kg) boned lamb shoulder
1 tablespoon sunflower oil
1 large onion, chopped
1 cup (8 fl oz/250 ml) water
3-in (7.5-cm) cinnamon stick
½ teaspoon ground allspice
½ teaspoon ground ginger
salt and freshly-ground black pepper
2 quinces, peeled, halved and cored
2 tablespoons butter
½ teaspoon ground cinnamon
pinch ground cloves
3 tablespoons sugar
lemon juice to taste

Trim excess fat from lamb and cut into 1-in (2.5-cm) cubes. Heat oil in a large heavy-based saucepan. Working in batches, add lamb cubes and cook over high heat until browned all over. Transfer to a plate, and repeat until all lamb is cooked then set aside.

Reduce heat, add onion to saucepan and cook gently until softened, about 5 minutes. Add water and stir well to lift browned juices. Return lamb to pan and add cinnamon stick, allspice, ginger, and salt and pepper to taste. Cover and simmer for 1 hour.

Cut each quince half into quarters. Melt butter in a frying pan, add quinces and cook over medium heat for several minutes, turning pieces. Sprinkle with ground cinnamon, cloves and sugar, and place on top of lamb in pan. Cover pan and simmer until lamb is tender, about 30 minutes, gently shaking pan occasionally. Add lemon juice to taste and adjust seasoning if necessary. Serve hot.

# Lamb tagine with dried fruits
## Tagine el ain
ALGERIA

When dates are being dried, they exude a thick molasses-like syrup. Dried dates soaked and pureed and the addition of brown sugar give a similar flavor.

**Serves** 5–6
**Cooking time** 1¾ hours

2 lb (1 kg) boneless lamb stew meat
2–3 tablespoons ghee or oil
1 medium-sized onion, chopped
2 cups (16 fl oz/500 ml) water
salt and freshly-ground black pepper to taste
3-in (7.5-cm) cinnamon stick
1 teaspoon ground ginger
½ teaspoon ground cumin
thinly-peeled zest (rind) of ½ lemon
¾ cup (4 oz/125 g) dried apricots
¾ cup (4 oz/125 g) dried prunes, pitted
½ cup (3 oz/90 g) raisins
1 tablespoon orange flower water
2 tablespoons brown sugar

Cut meat into ¾-in (2-cm) cubes. Heat half of ghee or oil in a heavy-based pan. Add meat, and cook until browned all over.

Push meat to one side, add onion and cook for 5 minutes. Reduce heat and add 1 cup (8 fl oz/250 ml) water, salt and pepper to taste, cinnamon stick, ginger, cumin and lemon zest. Cover and simmer for 1 hour.

Add apricots, prunes, raisins, orange flower water and sugar to meat. Stir, cover tightly and simmer until lamb is tender, a further 30 minutes. Check during cooking to ensure fruit does not catch, adding a little more water if necessary.

Remove cinnamon and lemon zest, and serve hot with rice.

VARIATION: Sprinkle with toasted almonds, slivered, whole or flaked, before serving.

# Beef tagine with prunes
## Lham tagine bil barkook
MOROCCO

**Serves** 6
**Cooking time** 2¼ hours

2 lb (1 kg) chuck or blade steak
2 tablespoons butter
2 tablespoons oil
1 onion, chopped
½ teaspoon ground ginger
2 cinnamon sticks
1½ cups (12 fl oz/375 ml) water
¼ teaspoon powdered saffron
4 sprigs cilantro (fresh coriander), tied together
salt and freshly-ground black pepper
thinly-peeled zest (rind) of ½ lemon
1½ cups (9 oz/280 g) pitted prunes
2 teaspoons rose water
2 tablespoons honey
2 tablespoons toasted slivered almonds

Trim beef and cut into 1-in (2.5-cm) cubes. In a heavy-based saucepan over high heat, heat butter and 1 tablespoon oil. Add beef in batches and cook, turning, until brown all over. Remove to a plate and repeat until all beef is cooked, adding remaining oil as needed, then set aside.

Reduce heat to medium, add onion to pan and cook gently until softened, about 5 minutes. Add ginger and cinnamon sticks, and cook for about 1 minute. Add water, saffron and cilantro sprigs, season with salt and pepper to taste, and stir well. Return beef to pan, stir, cover and simmer over low heat for 1½ hours.

Stir in lemon zest, prunes, rose water and honey, cover and simmer until beef is tender, a further 30 minutes. Remove lemon zest and cilantro, and discard. Serve sprinkled with toasted slivered almonds.

NOTE: For a more exciting flavor, add 1½ teaspoons Spice Blend (page 18), in place of ginger and cinnamon.

# Meatball tagine with tomato and eggs Kefta mkaouara

MOROCCO

**Serves** 4
**Cooking time** 55–60 minutes

1 small onion, grated
1 tablespoon finely-chopped fresh flat-leaf (Italian) parsley
1 tablespoon finely-chopped cilantro (fresh coriander)
¾ cup (1½ oz/45 g) soft white bread crumbs
1 lb (500 g) finely-ground (minced) lamb or beef
½ teaspoon ground cumin
½ teaspoon paprika
pinch cayenne pepper
1 teaspoon salt
oil for frying
4–6 eggs

For tomato sauce:
1 onion, finely chopped
1 clove garlic, crushed
1 teaspoon ground cumin
1 teaspoon ground cinnamon
½ teaspoon Harissa (page 20) or ¼ teaspoon cayenne pepper
14-oz (425-g) can tomatoes, chopped
2 tablespoons tomato paste
½ cup (4 fl oz/125 ml) water
1 tablespoon chopped fresh flat-leaf (Italian) parsley
2 tablespoons chopped cilantro (fresh coriander)
½ teaspoon sugar
salt and freshly-ground black pepper

In a bowl, mix onion, parsley, cilantro and bread crumbs. Add ground lamb or beef, cumin, paprika, cayenne pepper and salt. Mix well, then knead thoroughly with hands until paste-like in consistency.

With moistened hands, shape meatball mixture into walnut-sized balls and place on a tray. Heat a large, nonstick frying pan with lid to fit, and add oil to just cover base. Add meatballs and fry over high heat, turning to brown evenly. Remove using a slotted spoon, drain on paper towels and set aside.

To make tomato sauce: Drain oil from frying pan, reserving about 1 tablespoon. Add onion and cook over low heat for 5 minutes. Stir in garlic, cumin, cinnamon and harissa, and cook for 30 seconds. Stir in tomatoes, tomato paste, water, parsley, cilantro and sugar, and season with salt and pepper to taste. Cover and simmer for 10 minutes. Return meatballs to pan, cover and simmer over low heat for 30 minutes.

Move meatballs in pan into serving-sized groups. Break required number of eggs into spaces. Cover and simmer until eggs are set. Serve from pan at table.

# Meat with taro Kolkas

## EGYPT

Only the Egyptians use taro in their regional cooking. They call both the root and the dish it is used in "kolkas." See Ingredients (page 15) for information on taro: remember not to wet the root once peeled and cut as it can go slimy.

**Serves** 6
**Cooking time** 2¼ hours

2 lb (1 kg) boneless stewing lamb or beef
¼ cup (2 oz/60 g) butter
1½ cups (12 fl oz/375 ml) water
salt
freshly-ground black pepper
2 lb (1 kg) taro
juice of ½ lemon
15 Swiss chard (silverbeet) leaves
1 tablespoon finely-chopped cilantro (fresh coriander) leaves
2 cloves garlic, crushed

Trim lamb or beef and cut into cubes.

Melt 1 tablespoon butter in a large, deep saucepan and fry meat lightly, just enough for it to lose red color; do not brown. Add water, about 2 teaspoons salt and pepper to taste, and stir. Cover and simmer gently until half-cooked, about 1 hour.

Wash taro and dry well. Peel and cut into squarish pieces about ¾ in (2 cm) thick. Add taro and lemon juice to meat in pan; make sure taro pieces are completely immersed in liquid otherwise they could discolor. Cover and simmer until meat is tender, a further 1 hour. Do not stir once taro is added.

Wash chard well and strip leaves from white stalks (stalks can be used as a vegetable for later meals). Drain leaves.

Heat remaining butter in a large frying pan and add chard. Stir over medium heat until well wilted and darkened in color.

Chop finely while in pan, add cilantro and garlic, and cook, stirring, for 1 minute.

Add chard mixture to cooked meat, cover pan and remove pan from heat. Let stand for 5 minutes before serving. Serve with bread.

**Meat**

# Spiced roast lamb Mechoui

## MOROCCO, ALGERIA, TUNISIA

**A feature of Berber feasts, popular in the countries of the Maghreb. At moussems (festivals), whole lamb is spit-roasted over a pit of glowing coals and frequently basted until it is meltingly tender.**

**Serves** 6
**Cooking time** 3 hours

1 leg lamb, about 4 lb (2 kg)
3 cloves garlic, chopped
½ teaspoon salt
4 teaspoons ground coriander
2 teaspoons ground cumin
1 teaspoon paprika
¼ teaspoon cayenne pepper
3 tablespoons soft butter or ghee
watercress sprigs for garnish
1½ tablespoons ground cumin mixed with
   2 teaspoons sea salt for serving

With point of a knife, make deep incisions in lamb. Put chopped garlic in a mortar, add salt and pound to a paste using a pestle. Mix in coriander, cumin, paprika and cayenne pepper then using pestle work in butter to make a paste. Insert some of paste into incisions, place lamb in a baking pan and spread remaining paste all over lamb with a pallet knife. Cover with plastic wrap and marinate for 2 hours; refrigerate in hot weather.

Preheat oven to 350°F (180°C/Gas 4). Bake lamb on center shelf for 1½ hours. After first 30 minutes, baste lamb with fat in pan and reduce oven temperature to 325°F (170°C/Gas 3). Bake for a further 1½ hours, basting every 20 minutes to keep lamb moist. The moderately-low temperatures and long cooking browns the lamb without burning the spices, and cooks it to melting tenderness. Lamb must be well-done; an instant-read meat thermometer inserted into thickest part of lamb should read 175°F (80°C).

Serve lamb on a platter garnished with watercress. Carve at table and place small dishes of cumin and salt mixture within reach of diners for adding according to individual taste.

# Lamb kebabs Quotban
## MOROCCO

There are many versions of kebabs in the Greater Maghreb, some combine lamb with kidney or liver, a few use lamb only. In Morocco, they add small cubes of lamb tail fat between the lamb cubes; beef suet is often given as a substitute as lambs outside the region are of other breeds. Serve kebabs in warm bread with salads, pickles and olives served separately.

**Serves** 6

2 lb (1 kg) boneless lamb leg meat
½ cup (4 fl oz/125 ml) fresh lemon juice
4 tablespoons olive oil
2 teaspoons shredded fresh ginger
3 cloves garlic, crushed
½ teaspoon ground allspice
¼ teaspoon cayenne pepper
freshly-ground black pepper
salt

Trim excess fat from lamb and cut into ¾-in (2-cm) cubes. Combine lamb, lemon juice, oil, ginger, garlic, allspice, cayenne pepper and black pepper in a bowl. Stir well, cover and refrigerate for at least 2 hours or overnight, stirring occasionally.

Thread lamb onto skewers and cook over glowing coals on barbecue, basting frequently with marinade. Cook to pink stage, or well-done if preferred; do not overcook or lamb will toughen. Season with salt after cooking, if desired. Serve hot, on skewers.

# Ground meat kebabs Kefta kebab
## MOROCCO, TUNISIA, ALGERIA

This is street food in the Maghreb, served in bread with an extra sprinkling of salt and cumin, but I like to add salad vegetables. Purchase meat that is not too lean. If you are using long skewers, have two portions of meat mixture on each skewer. Use one portion on short skewers. To cook the kebabs, remove the grid from the barbecue if possible and place skewers so that the ends rest on the sides of the barbecue. A Habachi barbecue is ideal for cooking these.

**Serves** 6
**Cooking time** 6–8 minutes

2 lb (1 kg) finely ground (minced) lamb or beef
4 tablespoons chopped fresh flat-leaf (Italian)
  parsley
2 tablespoons chopped cilantro (fresh
  coriander) leaves
1 small onion, chopped
1½ teaspoons salt
freshly-ground black pepper
½ teaspoon ground allspice
¼ teaspoon cayenne pepper
1 teaspoon ground cumin
1 teaspoon paprika
olive oil
pita or other flat bread, warmed, for serving
Harissa (page 20) for serving

Place meat, parsley, coriander, onion, salt, pepper to taste, and spices in a bowl. Pass through meat grinder (mincer) twice using a fine screen, or process in 4 batches in a food processor. Knead to a smooth paste by hand if grinder is used; if processed, knead to blend flavors evenly. Cover bowl and refrigerate for 30 minutes.

With moistened hands, take about 2 heaping tablespoons of meat paste and mold into 4-in (10-cm) long finger shapes around flat, sword-like skewers. As skewers are prepared, place across baking dish with ends of skewers resting on each side. Cover and refrigerate 1 hour.

Preheat barbecue. Brush kebabs lightly with oil and cook on barbecue until cooked through, 6–8 minutes, turning frequently.

To serve, slide kebabs off skewers and serve with warm bread and a little harissa.

# Spicy lamb sausages Merguez
## TUNISIA

These spicy sausages of Tunisia have found fame abroad. Also used in Morocco and Algeria, with a lighter touch of the fiery Tunisian harissa, French-Algerians took them to France, and they are now made by butchers there as well as in other countries. The sausages are broiled (grilled), fried or used in egg dishes. Don't try to reduce the salt—it is important in the binding process of the meat where the salt reacts with the myosin in the meat to create a natural binder—and use pure cooking salt, not table salt. Sausage fillers are available as attachments for some food processors and meat grinders. Special hand-held sausage fillers are also available. Purchase either fresh or dry collagen sausage casings from the butcher. Dry casings come already "shirred" into a cylinder shape. Store sausages loosely-covered in refrigerator 1 day before cooking for flavors to develop.

**Makes** about 3 lb (1.5 kg) sausages

3 lb (1.5 kg) boneless lamb leg or forequarter
  meat
3 teaspoons salt
1 teaspoon freshly-ground black pepper
2–3 teaspoons Harissa (page 20)
2 teaspoons ground fennel seeds
2 teaspoons ground coriander
2 tablespoons paprika
2 teaspoons ground cumin
1 teaspoon ground allspice
4 cloves garlic, finely chopped
1 cup (8 fl oz/250 ml) iced water
thin sausage casings

Trim any fine skin and thick gristle from lamb, but leave a good proportion of fat. Cut into ¾-in (2-cm) cubes; check weight. If lamb is not very cold after preparation, cover and refrigerate at least 2 hours in coldest part of refrigerator. Place lamb in a large bowl, sprinkle with salt and mix well. Process in 6 batches in a food processor with steel blade until finely ground (minced). Transfer to a wide dish and mix in pepper, harissa to taste, spices and garlic. Process again in 6 batches to mix evenly, adding 2–3 tablespoons iced water to each batch. Transfer to a large bowl and mix well with hand.

If sausage casings are fresh, rinse salt from casings and soak in warm water for 30 minutes. Run cold water through each length of casing to check for holes. Fit about 3 ft (1 m) of fresh casing onto nozzle of sausage filler or large funnel. If using dry casings, cut off 3-in (7.5-cm) length of shirred casing.

Pass lamb mixture through sausage filler or push through funnel with end of wooden spoon. When mixture appears at end of nozzle, stop and pull casing over nozzle. Tie casing, then continue with filling. Let sausage curl into dish. When casing is filled, leave open end unfilled and untied, and fill more casings as required.

Stretch sausage along work surface and press halfway point with finger. Twist at this point 3 times. Even out sausage between twist and tied end, mark halfway point and twist again. Then continue to twist at halfway points until required sausage lengths are formed. Twist in same manner toward untied end, smoothing out sausage after each twist. Tie off end.

Keep covered in refrigerator for up to 2 days, or wrap well and store in freezer.

Broil (grill), barbecue or fry sausages and serve with pita bread and salad, or with Peppers with Tomatoes and Eggs (Chakchouka) (page 102).

## Braised okra with tomatoes
## Marak matisha bil melokhias
MOROCCO

I like okra, providing its viscous sap has been reduced. While this recipe comes from Morocco, and is popular in other North African countries, the okra preparation before cooking is Greek, as this reduces the viscosity and prevents the okra from splitting. Serve as part of a Moroccan meal or as a separate dish, with couscous if desired.

**Serves** 6
**Cooking time** 50–55 minutes

1 lb (500 g) fresh okra
½ cup (4 fl oz/125 ml) distilled white vinegar
3 tablespoons olive oil
1 large onion, sliced
2 cloves garlic, chopped
2 x 14-oz (425-g) cans tomatoes, chopped but undrained
2 tablespoons chopped fresh flat-leaf (Italian) parsley
1 teaspoon paprika
salt and freshly-ground black pepper
extra chopped fresh parsley for serving

Wash okra and trim stalks but do not remove cone-shaped tops. Place in a bowl, pour over vinegar and turn with hand to coat. Let stand for 20 minutes. Drain okra then rinse well and dry gently with a clean cloth.

Heat oil in a saucepan. Add onion and garlic, and cook gently until onion is translucent, about 10 minutes. Stir in tomatoes with their liquid, parsley, paprika, and salt and pepper to taste. Simmer, stirring occasionally, over medium–low heat until thick, about 20 minutes.

Add okra, cover pan and simmer gently over low heat until okra is tender, about 20–25 minutes. Transfer carefully to serving dish and sprinkle with extra chopped parsley. Serve hot or at room temperature.

# Peppers with tomatoes and eggs
## Chakchouka
TUNISIA

**This is but one version of chakchouka prepared in the Greater Maghreb. Eggs are important in the cooking of this region as they are an inexpensive meat substitute. The number of eggs added depends on whether you are cooking a light snack or a main course. In Tunisia, the Spicy Lamb Sausages, Merguez (page 98), often feature in this dish but spicy Italian sausages can be used instead; prick 4 sausages and fry gently in an oiled frying pan until cooked through, cut into thick slices and add to recipe with the tomatoes.**

**Serves** 4
**Cooking time** 25 minutes

2 green bell peppers (capsicums)
1 red bell pepper (capsicum)
⅓ cup (3 fl oz/90 ml) olive oil
2 cloves garlic, finely chopped
3 medium-sized ripe tomatoes, peeled and
  chopped
1 teaspoon Harissa (page 20) or ¼ teaspoon
  cayenne pepper mixed with ½ teaspoon
  ground cumin
3 tablespoons chopped fresh flat-leaf (Italian)
  parsley
salt
4–8 eggs
paprika for garnish

Cut bell peppers in half, remove cores, seeds and membrane, then cut into ½-in (12-mm) strips. Heat oil in a large frying pan. Add bell pepper and stir over medium heat for 5 minutes. Add garlic and cook for several seconds. Stir in tomatoes, harissa or cayenne pepper–cumin mixture, parsley, and salt to taste, cover and simmer until vegetables are tender, about 15 minutes.

Remove lid, and make 4–8 hollows in vegetables for eggs. Break eggs into hollows, cover pan and simmer until eggs are cooked as desired. Sprinkle lightly with paprika, and serve hot with crusty bread.

# Bell peppers stuffed with chickpeas
## Felfa hlouwa mahshi bil hummus
### MOROCCO, ALGERIA

When meat is unavailable, pulses such as chickpeas substitute. These stuffed bell peppers show the Ottoman influence in north-eastern Morocco and the bordering coastal Algeria.

**Serves** 6
**Cooking time** about 1 hour

12 medium-sized green bell peppers
  (capsicums)

For chickpea and rice stuffing:
¼ cup (2 fl oz/60 ml) olive oil
6 scallions (shallots/spring onions), chopped
1 cup (7 oz/220 g) long-grain rice
14-oz (425-g) can chickpeas, drained
4 tablespoons chopped fresh flat-leaf (Italian)
  parsley
2 medium-sized tomatoes, peeled and chopped
½ teaspoon ground allspice
salt and freshly-ground black pepper

For tomato sauce:
2 tablespoons olive oil
1 medium onion, grated
1 clove garlic, crushed
1 cup (8 fl oz/250 ml) water or chicken stock
3 tablespoons tomato paste
1 teaspoon sugar
salt and freshly-ground black pepper to taste
2 tablespoons finely-chopped fresh flat-leaf
  (Italian) parsley

Cut tops from bell peppers, trim and reserve. Remove seeds and white membrane. Place bell peppers in a saucepan of boiling salted water and boil for 5 minutes. Remove using a slotted spoon and invert to drain on layers of paper towels.

To make chickpea and rice stuffing: Heat oil in a frying pan. Add scallions and cook gently for 2–3 minutes. Remove from heat, stir in remaining stuffing ingredients and season to taste with salt and pepper.

Preheat oven to 325–350°F (170–180°C/Gas 3–4). Oil or grease a baking dish. Place bell peppers upright in baking dish and fill loosely with stuffing. Replace tops of bell peppers.

To make tomato sauce: Warm oil in a small saucepan. Add onion and garlic, and cook gently for 5 minutes. Stir in remaining sauce ingredients and bring to a boil.

Pour tomato sauce over bell peppers, cover baking dish with lid or aluminum foil, and bake for 45 minutes. Remove from oven, uncover and bake for a further 15 minutes, basting bell peppers with sauce if necessary to keep them moist. Serve hot.

# Pumpkin stew Marak dar marhzin
## MOROCCO

A marak is a vegetable version of tagine, usually served as a separate course. The following recipe combines pumpkin with root vegetables and can be served with couscous, as suggested, or with boiled brown rice for a modern vegetarian dish.

**Serves 4–6**

3 tablespoons butter or oil
2 large onions, finely chopped
2 cloves garlic, finely chopped
1 teaspoon ground turmeric
1 teaspoon ground ginger
1 teaspoon ground cinnamon
2 medium carrots, sliced
2 small white turnips, peeled and cut into
   quarters (optional)
3 cups (24 fl oz/750 ml) water
1 lb (500 g) butternut pumpkin (squash), peeled
   and cubed
1 lb (500 g) sweet potato (kumara), peeled and
   cubed
1 teaspoon Harissa (page 20)
⅓ cup (2 oz/60 g) raisins
3 teaspoons honey
salt and freshly-ground black pepper
cilantro (fresh coriander) leaves for garnish
Basic Couscous (page 19) for serving
lime wedges for serving

Melt butter in a large heavy-based saucepan. Add onion and cook gently for 5 minutes. Add garlic, tumeric, ginger and cinnamon, and cook, stirring occasionally, for 2 minutes. Stir in carrots, turnips and water, and bring to a boil. Cover and simmer for 10 minutes. Add pumpkin, sweet potato, harissa, raisins, honey, and salt and pepper to taste. Cover and simmer until vegetables are tender, a further 20 minutes.

Transfer to a warm bowl and garnish with cilantro leaves. Alternatively, pile hot couscous onto a warm platter, make a hollow in center and ladle pumpkin stew into center.

Serve with lime wedges in a separate bowl, to be squeezed on according to individual taste.

VARIATION: Add 14-oz (425-g) can chickpeas, drained and rinsed, with pumpkin to give finished stew more substance, if desired.

# Date-filled pastries Magrood

LIBYA

**Makes** 30
**Cooking time** 20–25 minutes

3 cups (15 oz/470 g) all-purpose (plain) flour
½ cup (3½ oz/110 g) superfine (caster) sugar
1 cup (8 oz/250 g) unsalted butter
3 teaspoons orange flower water or rose water
¼ cup (2 fl oz/60 ml) water
confectioners' (icing) sugar for coating

For date filling:
1⅓ cups (8 oz (250 g) pitted dates
2 tablespoons butter

Sift flour and sugar into a large mixing bowl. Cut butter into pieces and rub into flour with fingertips until distributed evenly.

Blend orange flower water with water and sprinkle onto flour mixture. Mix to a firm dough and knead lightly until smooth. Set aside to rest for 30 minutes.

Meanwhile to make filling: Chop dates, place in a saucepan with butter and heat gently until dates soften, stirring often. Remove pan from heat and set aside.

Preheat oven to 325°F (170°C/Gas 3).

Taking about 1 tablespoon dough at a time, roll into a ball the size of a large walnut. Flatten ball in palm of your hand and place 1 teaspoon date filling in center.

Mold dough around filling and reshape into a ball. Place on an ungreased baking sheet, flatten slightly and press tines of fork obliquely around sides and across top, giving pastries a slightly conical shape. Repeat with remaining ingredients.

Bake pastries until lightly colored, 20–25 minutes. Remove from oven and let cool on baking sheets for 10 minutes.

Sift some confectioners' sugar onto a sheet of waxed (greaseproof) paper. Place pastries on sugar and sift more sugar on top to coat lightly. When cool, store in an airtight container.

# Rice pudding Roz bil halib

## MOROCCO, ALGERIA, TUNISIA, LIBYA

**Serves** 6–8

½ cup (3½ oz/110 g) medium-grain rice
1 cup (8 fl oz/250 ml) water
pinch salt
4½ cups (36 fl oz/1.1 L) milk
¼ cup (2 oz/60 g) sugar
2 tablespoons cornstarch (cornflour)
1 tablespoon orange flower water or rose
   water
chopped toasted almonds or pistachio nuts for
   serving

Put rice in a large, heavy-based saucepan with water and salt. Place over medium heat and cook, stirring occasionally, until water is absorbed, about 5–6 minutes. Reserve ½ cup (4 fl oz/125 ml) milk and set aside. Add remaining milk to rice, stir well and bring to a slow simmer. Cook for 25–30 minutes, stirring occasionally. Be careful pudding does not boil over. Pudding is cooked when rice is very soft; test a grain occasionally. When rice is cooked, stir in sugar.

Mix cornstarch with reserved milk and gradually pour into pudding, stirring constantly. Cook, stirring constantly, until thickened, then boil gently for 2 minutes. Remove pan from heat and stir in orange flower water or rose water. Let stand for a few minutes to cool, stirring occasionally to prevent a skin forming.

Pour into individual bowls. Refrigerate to chill if desired, but this is usually served at room temperature. Sprinkle with chopped toasted almonds or pistachio nuts (untoasted).

VARIATION: This pudding is delicious served with dried fruits such as apricots or prunes that have been poached in a sugar syrup with a cinnamon stick or dash of orange flower water or rose water for typical Maghrebi flavors.

# Watermelon with rose water
## Dalah bi ma'el ward
MOROCCO

**Serves** 4

3 lb (1.5 kg) wedge of watermelon
1 tablespoon rose water
fresh mint sprigs

Remove skin from watermelon so that base of wedge is flat. Cut watermelon into 1-in (2.5-cm) thick slices to resemble tall triangles. Arrange on a platter with points up. Using end of a teaspoon, drizzle rose water over watermelon, cover and refrigerate to chill.

Scatter with fresh mint sprigs or small leaves, and serve immediately.

# Sweet couscous with dates and nuts
## Farkha
TUNISIA

**Serves** 5–6
**Cooking time** 30 minutes

2 cups (12 oz/375 g) couscous
½ cup (3½ oz/110 g) superfine (caster) sugar
3 cups (24 fl oz/750 ml) boiling water
½ cup (4 oz/125 g) unsalted butter, chopped
1 cup (5 oz/150 g) chopped mixed nuts (blanched almonds, pistachio nuts, walnuts, pine nuts, hazelnuts)
8 oz (250 g) dessert dates, pitted and chopped
2 cups (16 fl oz/500 ml) milk, heated, for serving
superfine (caster) sugar for serving

Preheat oven to 350°F (180°C/Gas 4).

Put couscous and sugar in a baking pan, stir well to combine then spread evenly and dot with butter. Pour boiling water over couscous and butter, stir well, spread out again evenly and cover with aluminum foil. Let stand for 10 minutes.

Meanwhile spread nuts on a baking sheet and bake until fragrant and lightly toasted, 6–8 minutes. Tip into a large, shallow bowl.

Using a fork, fluff couscous well to break up lumps, replace foil cover and place in oven for 20 minutes to steam. This swells couscous further, making it lighter. Remove from oven, carefully remove foil, and fluff up again with a fork, breaking up any lumps.

Add hot couscous to nuts in bowl, add dates and toss lightly to combine. Serve hot in bowls, with hot milk served in a pitcher and extra sugar to be added to individual taste.

# Filo and milk pudding Om ali
EGYPT

This pudding combining filo pastry with milk, cream, nuts and raisins has become popular in Egypt in recent years. The name means "Mother of Ali."

**Serves** 6–8
**Cooking time** 55 minutes

8 oz (250 g) filo (phyllo) pastry, about
   12–14 sheets
⅓ cup (3 oz/90 g) unsalted butter, melted
½ cup (2½ oz/75 g) slivered almonds
⅓ cup (1½ oz/45 g) chopped pistachio nuts
⅓ cup (1½ oz/45 g) chopped hazelnuts
½ cup (3 oz/90 g) raisins
3 cups (24 fl oz/750 ml) whole milk
½ cup (4 oz/125 g) sugar
1½ cups (12 fl oz/375 ml) double (heavy) cream
3 teaspoons orange flower water
ground cinnamon for dusting

Preheat oven to 350°F (180°C/Gas 4). Grease 2 baking sheets. Brush filo sheets lightly with melted butter and form into 2 equal stacks on baking sheets; if filo sheets are too long, cut off excess and place on another baking sheet. Bake until crisp and lightly golden on top, about 10 minutes. Remove from oven and set aside to cool.

In a ceramic or glass baking dish about 13 x 9 x 2 in (33 x 23 x 5 cm) in size, arrange 1 filo stack, breaking sheets to fit if necessary and adding all broken pieces to dish. Press filo down into dish. Combine almonds, pistachio nuts and hazelnuts, and sprinkle half over filo with half of raisins. Top with remaining stack of filo as before.

Heat milk in a saucepan with sugar and stir until sugar is dissolved. Stir in cream and orange flower water. Pour evenly over filo in dish. Sprinkle remaining nuts and raisins on top and dust top lightly with ground cinnamon.

Bake until pudding is set and puffed, about 45 minutes; filo should absorb the liquid. Serve hot or warm.

# Figs with pistachios and honey Kermusat bi pistash wa'assel
## MOROCCO

**Serves** 6

12 fresh purple-skinned figs
⅓ cup (1½ oz/45 g) pistachio nuts
3 teaspoons orange flower water
1–2 tablespoons honey

Carefully wash figs and dry with paper towels. Place in refrigerator to chill. Cut off stems then cut each fig into quarters from stem end almost to base. Peel skin of each section almost down to base and curl down like petals. Gently open top of each fig and arrange on serving platter.

Chop pistachio nuts coarsely and set aside.

Using end of a teaspoon, drizzle a little orange flower water into center of each fig and sprinkle each with 1 teaspoon chopped pistachio nuts. Drizzle a little honey over nuts and serve immediately.

# Date sweetmeats Halawa tamr
## MOROCCO, ALGERIA, TUNISIA, LIBYA

**The country-dwelling Berbers and desert nomads region make many simple sweetmeats from their produce that do not require cooking but keep well. These are an example. Of course, they pound them in a mortar using a pestle.**

**Makes** About 40

1⅓ cups (8 oz/250 g) pitted dates
1⅓ cups (8 oz/250 g) dessert figs
2 teaspoons aniseed
2 tablespoons honey
1½ cups (7 oz/220 g) chopped mixed nuts (toasted blanched almonds and/or hazelnuts, walnuts, peanuts)
confectioners' (icing) sugar or toasted sesame seeds for coating

Chop dates and figs roughly and place in a food processor. Pound aniseed to a powder in a mortar using a pestle, or use a spice grinder. Add aniseed and honey to fruit, and process until a coarse paste is formed. Turn out into a bowl.

Add chopped mixed nuts to date mixture in bowl, and mix using a wooden spoon.

Place confectioners' sugar or toasted sesame seeds into a flat dish. Rub palms of hands with a little butter. Take 1 heaping teaspoon of date mixture and roll into a ball. Drop into dish of sugar or sesame seeds. Repeat until dish is full of balls. Clean and dry hands and roll balls in sugar or sesame seeds to coat. Transfer to a wire rack to dry a little. Repeat until all date mixture is rolled and coated. Store in an airtight container.

NOTE: Dessert figs are softer than normal dried figs and are easier to process.

# Fresh fruit platter Fakya
## MOROCCO, ALGERIA, TUNISIA

**Fresh fruit is served at the end of a meal. For banquets, it is beautifully arranged, sometimes with ice to keep it cool.**

**fresh fruit in season**
**fresh mint sprigs or leaves for garnish**

Prepare fruit so that it is easy to eat using hands: present grapes in small bunches; cut figs in halves or quarters; slice melons; cut stone fruits in half; peel and slice oranges, apples or pears. Rose water or orange flower water can be sprinkled on cut surfaces. Arrange on a platter and garnish with mint sprigs or leaves.

# Semolina cake Basbousa

## EGYPT, LIBYA

**Cooking time** 30–35 minutes

½ cup (4 oz/125 g) butter, preferably unsalted
¾ cup (6 oz/185 g) superfine (caster) sugar
1 teaspoon vanilla extract (essence)
2 eggs
2 cups (10 oz/300 g) fine semolina
1 teaspoon baking powder
½ teaspoon baking soda
¾ cup (6 fl oz/180 ml) plain (natural) whole-
   milk yogurt
blanched almonds, preferable halved (split)
whipped cream for garnish (optional)

**For syrup:**
2 cups (1 lb/500 g) sugar
1½ cups (12 fl oz/375 ml) water
1 tablespoon lemon juice

Preheat oven to 350°F (180°C/Gas 4).

In a bowl, cream butter, sugar and vanilla until light and fluffy. Add eggs, one at a time, beating well after each addition.

Sift semolina, baking powder and baking soda twice. Fold into butter mixture alternately with yogurt.

Spread batter into a greased 8- x 12-in (20- x 30-cm) cake pan. Arrange almonds evenly on top in rows (4 across width and 7 along length) so that when cake is cut, an almond will be centered on each piece.

Bake until top of cake springs back when pressed, 30–35 minutes.

Meanwhile, to make syrup: Place sugar and water in a heavy-based saucepan. Cook over medium heat, stirring occasionally, until sugar is dissolved. Add lemon juice and bring to a boil. Boil rapidly for 10 minutes, then cool by standing pan in cold water.

Spoon cooled syrup over hot cake. Cool thoroughly and cut into diamond shapes or squares to serve. Garnish with whipped cream if desired.

# Sweet couscous with nuts
## Couscous bi sukkar
EGYPT

**Serves** 6–8
**Cooking time** 45 minutes

2 cups (12 oz/375 g) Couscous (page 54) or
   instant couscous
water
½ cup (4 fl oz/125 ml) melted, unsalted butter

**For serving:**
**confectioners' (icing) sugar**
**toasted peanuts or almond slivers**

Put couscous in a bowl and cover with cold water. Stir with fingers then drain off water. Let stand for 15 minutes. Grains will swell.

Place couscous in top section of a couscoussier, set over 4 cups (32 fl oz/1 L) boiling water. Alternatively, place couscous in a fine sieve or colander lined with muslin (cheesecloth) which fits snugly over a deep saucepan of boiling water, ensuring that bottom of sieve or colander does not touch water.

Drape a kitchen towel over top of couscous container and fit lid on, bringing ends of cloth over top of lid. Steam for 15 minutes, then turn out couscous into a bowl. Break up any lumps with fingers or a fork and sprinkle with 2 tablespoons cold water. Fluff up with fork and return to steaming container, adding more boiling water if necessary.

Cover as before and steam for a further 30 minutes, or 20 minutes for instant couscous, regulating heat so that water boils gently. When cooking is completed, couscous should be tender without being mushy.

Turn out into a bowl and fluff up couscous with fork, breaking up any lumps. Add melted butter and toss through to coat grains evenly.

Serve warm, piled in individual dessert dishes, sprinkled with confectioners' sugar and peanuts or almonds.

# Nut shortbread cookies Ghorayebah

## MOROCCO, ALGERIA, TUNISIA, LIBYA

**Makes** about 40

1 cup (8 oz/250 g) unsalted butter
1 cup (4 oz/125 g) confectioners' (icing) sugar
1 egg yolk
1 tablespoon orange flower water
½ cup (2½ oz/75 g) finely-chopped skinned
   toasted hazelnuts or almonds (optional)
2½ cups (12½ oz/390 g) all-purpose (plain)
   flour
1 teaspoon baking powder
about 40 whole blanched almonds (optional)

Cream butter and confectioners' sugar until very light and fluffy. Beat in egg yolk and orange flower water, then fold in nuts if using. Sift flour with baking powder and fold into butter mixture to form soft dough. Press with finger; dough should not stick, otherwise mix in more flour.

Preheat oven to 300–325°F (150–170°C/ Gas 2–3). Lightly grease baking sheets.

Taking about 1 tablespoon dough, roll into a walnut-sized ball and place on baking sheet. Repeat with remaining dough, allowing room on baking sheet for spreading. Press thumb in middle of each ball to flatten slightly and to make indent. Place almond in center, if chopped nuts were not used. Bake until only lightly browned, about 15–20 minutes; do not overbrown or flavor will be altered. Let cool completely on baking sheets. Remove carefully with metal spatula and store in an airtight container.

# Almond pastry "snake" M'hanncha

MOROCCO

**Serves** 8
**Cooking time** 30–35 minutes

8–11 filo (phyllo) pastry sheets
½ cup (4 oz/125 g) unsalted butter, melted
1 egg yolk
confectioners' (icing) sugar for dusting
ground cinnamon

**For almond filling:**
1 egg white
2½ cups (10 oz/300 g) ground almonds
¾ cup (3 oz/90 g) confectioners' (icing) sugar
2 tablespoons butter, melted
¼ teaspoon almond extract (essence)
1½ tablespoons orange flower water

Leave filo pastry in packaging at room temperature for 1–2 hours before using. Lightly butter a 9-in (23-cm) springform cake pan. Preheat oven to 180°C (350°F/Gas 4).

To make filling: Lightly beat egg white in a bowl and mix in remaining filling ingredients to form a paste. Cover and refrigerate to chill for 30 minutes. Mold filling into a thick roll and cut into 12–15 even slices (see Note below). Roll each slice into a cylinder ½ in (1 cm) in diameter and set aside on a tray.

Stack 11 filo pastry sheets and cover with a folded kitchen towel to prevent drying. Seal and store remainder. Keep melted butter warm by placing pan in hot water. Place 1 filo sheet on work surface with longer edge toward you. Brush with butter, then cover with another sheet, brushing top with butter. Place 3 filling cylinders side by side ½ in (1 cm) in from bottom edge and sides of filo, placing them close together to form a single roll. Turn bottom edge of filo over filling, fold in sides and roll to end of filo. Form into a coil and place coil, seam-side down, in center of springform pan. Repeat to make 3 or 4 more pastry rolls to extend coil and fill pan. If coil breaks, cut small pieces of remaining filo sheet, brush with a little egg yolk and press onto breaks.

Brush coil with remaining egg yolk and bake until golden-brown, 30–35 minutes. Remove side of pan and slide pastry onto a wire rack. When warm, dust with extra confectioners' sugar and sprinkle cinnamon in a lattice pattern on top. Serve warm or cold. Pastry can be cut in wedges, or break off portions as required. May be stored in an airtight container at room temperature for up to 3 days.

NOTE: Make an extra roll if filo pastry length is less than 15 in (38 cm).

# Almond cream pudding Muhallabia
## TUNISIA

**Also known as Mulhalabya, this pudding is found across North Africa.**

**Serves** 6

**3 tablespoons ground rice**
**3 cups (24 fl oz/750 ml) milk**
**pinch salt**
**¼ cup (2 oz/60 g) sugar**
**¾ cup (3 oz/90 g) ground blanched almonds**
**1 tablespoon rose water**
**chopped pistachio nuts or almonds for garnish**
**pomegranate seeds (optional)**

In a small bowl, mix ground rice with ¼ cup (2 fl oz/60 ml) milk.

Bring remaining milk to a boil in a heavy-based saucepan. Stir in ground rice mixture, salt and sugar. Reduce heat to medium and cook, stirring constantly with a wooden spoon, until mixture bubbles gently. Reduce heat to low and simmer for 5 minutes, stirring often so mixture cooks slowly and does not scorch.

Stir in ground almonds until blended smoothly, then add rose water. Remove pan from heat and stir occasionally until mixture cools slightly.

Pour into a serving bowl or 6 individual dessert bowls or glasses. Refrigerate to chill. Serve garnished with chopped nuts and pomegranate seeds if using.

# Gazelle's horns Kaab el ghzal
## MOROCCO, ALGERIA, TUNISIA

**Instead of orange flower water and confectioners' sugar, uncooked pastries may be glazed with beaten egg and a little milk. Cut slits in pastry after glazing then bake as described below.**

**Makes** about 30
**Cooking time** 15 minutes per batch

2 cups (10 oz/300 g) all-purpose (plain) flour
1 tablespoon butter, melted
1 egg yolk
2 tablespoons orange flower water
about ½ cup (4 fl oz/125 ml) cold water

**For almond filling:**
2½ cups (14 oz/425 g) whole blanched almonds
¾ cup (3 oz/90 g) confectioners' (icing) sugar
1 tablespoon orange flower water
1 egg white
2 tablespoons butter, melted
½ teaspoon ground cinnamon
¼ teaspoon almond extract (essence)

⅓ cup (3 fl oz/90 ml) orange flower water for coating
1 cup (4 oz/125 g) confectioners' (icing) sugar, sifted, for coating

Place flour, butter, egg yolk, orange flower water and half of cold water in a food processor. Process until dough forms on blades. If still crumbly, slowly add remaining water. Process for a further 1 minute to make elastic. Turn out dough and knead until smooth. Divide in half, wrap in plastic wrap and let stand at least 15 minutes.

To make almond filling: Place almonds in clean food processor with sugar, and process until almonds are finely ground. Add remaining ingredients and process to a stiff paste. Taking about 3 teaspoons paste at a time, shape into balls then mold into cylinders about 3 in (7.5 cm) long and tapering slightly at each end. Place on a tray and set aside.

Grease a baking tray. Preheat oven to 325–350°F (160–180°C/Gas 3–4).

Roll out half of dough on floured work surface into a 12- x 16-in (30- x 40-cm) rectangle, with longer edge toward you. Place 3 filling cylinders on pastry, 2 in (5 cm) up from lower edge, and 1½ in (4 cm) apart and from each end. Lightly brush lower edge of pastry and in between filling with water. Fold bottom of pastry over filling, molding and pressing around each cylinder to seal. With fluted pastry wheel, cut around filling into a semicircle, making a ¾-in (2-cm) border. Remove pastries and press cut edge again to firmly seal. Pick up each pastry, filling-side up, and bend up into crescent shape. Place on baking tray. Make 3 tiny diagonal slits in top of pastries with point of sharp knife.

Cut edge of remaining pastry on board with knife to straighten, then fill and shape again. Repeat with remaining half of dough, using pastry trimmings as well. Bake until lightly colored, about 15 minutes.

Place orange flower water in a small bowl and confectioners' sugar in a deep bowl. Working quickly while pastries are hot, dip each into orange flower water then drop into bowl of sugar. Using dry hand, coat pastry with sugar and set aside on wire rack to cool. Repeat to coat all pastries. Sift more sugar over cooled pastries and store in an airtight container at room temperature.

# drinks

## Mint tea Chay na'na
### MOROCCO, ALGERIA, TUNISIA

In Morocco, mint tea preparation can take on an air of ceremony, presided over by the head of the household. All the requirements are set out on a decorated brass tray-table—teapot (bulbous-shaped with a domed lid), tea, fresh mint and sugar in containers, and decorative tea glasses. The sugar is a solid cone about 8 in (20 cm) high, with pieces broken off with a brass hammer.

**Serves** 4, allowing 2 glasses per serve

6–8 leafy sprigs fresh spearmint (*Mentha spicata*)
1 tablespoon green tea, preferably Formosan gunpowder
¼ cup (2 oz/60 g) sugar
boiling water

Cut off ends of mint stems that have no leaves and discard. Pinch off 4 top sprigs and set aside. Lightly crush mint.

Rinse a 4-cup (24-fl oz/1-L) teapot with boiling water. Add tea, sugar and mint to pot and pour in boiling water. Cover with lid and let brew for 3 minutes, stirring once. Pour out a glass of tea then return to pot to further blend infusion.

Place reserved mint sprigs in 4 tea glasses and pour in tea from a height; this aerates it making surface frothy. Glasses are filled almost to the brim.

To drink, grip rim of glass with thumb and forefinger of right hand, and sip.

# Almond milk drink Sharbat bil looz

## MOROCCO

**Makes** 6–8 glasses

2 cups (11 oz/340 g) blanched almonds
⅓ cup (2½ oz/75 g) superfine (caster) sugar
1½ cups (12 fl oz/375 ml) hot water
½ cup (4 fl oz/125 ml) cold water
¼ teaspoon almond extract (essence)
1 teaspoon rose water
1 cup (8 fl oz/250 ml) cold milk

Place almonds in a blender or food processor with sugar and most of hot water. Let stand for 10 minutes to soften almonds, then blend or process until almonds are well pulverized.

Pour through a fine-meshed sieve set over a bowl. Rinse blender or food processor with remaining hot water and pour through sieve. Press with back of a spoon to extract moisture. Add cold water to almonds in sieve, mix through and press again with back of a spoon to extract all "milk." Discard almonds.

Stir almond extract, rose water and milk into almond milk. Taste and stir in extra sugar if necessary. Pour into a pitcher, cover and refrigerate to chill for 2 hours. Serve in small glasses.

# index

# guide to weights and measures

The metric weights and metric fluid measures used in this book are those of Standards Australia. All cup and spoon measurements are level:
- The Australian Standard measuring cup has a capacity of 250 millilitres (250 ml).
- The Australian Standard tablespoon has a capacity of 20 millilitres (20 ml).

In all recipes metric equivalents of imperial measures are shown in parentheses e.g. 1 lb (500 g) beef. For successful cooking use either metric or imperial weights and measures—do not mix the two.

## Weights

| Imperial | Metric |
|---|---|
| 1/3 oz | 10 g |
| 1/2 oz | 15 g |
| 3/4 oz | 20 g |
| 1 oz | 30 g |
| 2 oz | 60 g |
| 3 oz | 90 g |
| 4 oz (1/4 lb) | 125 g |
| 5 oz (1/3 lb) | 150 g |
| 6 oz | 180 g |
| 7 oz | 220 g |
| 8 oz (1/2 lb) | 250 g |
| 9 oz | 280 g |
| 10 oz | 300 g |
| 11 oz | 330 g |
| 12 oz (3/4 lb) | 375 g |
| 16 oz (1 lb) | 500 g |
| 2 lb | 1 kg |
| 3 lb | 1.5 kg |
| 4 lb | 2 kg |

## Volume

| Imperial | Metric | Cup |
|---|---|---|
| 1 fl oz | 30 ml | |
| 2 fl oz | 60 ml | 1/4 |
| 3 fl oz | 90 ml | 1/3 |
| 4 fl oz | 125 ml | 1/2 |
| 5 fl oz | 150 ml | 2/3 |
| 6 fl oz | 180 ml | 3/4 |
| 8 fl oz | 250 ml | 1 |
| 10 fl oz | 300 ml | 1 1/4 |
| 12 fl oz | 375 ml | 1 1/2 |
| 13 fl oz | 400 ml | 1 2/3 |
| 14 fl oz | 440 ml | 1 3/4 |
| 16 fl oz | 500 ml | 2 |
| 24 fl oz | 750 ml | 3 |
| 32 fl oz | 1 L | 4 |

## Oven temperature guide

The Celsius (°C) and Fahrenheit (°F) temperatures in this chart apply to most electric ovens. Decrease by 25°F or 10°C for a gas oven or refer to the manufacturer's temperature guide. For temperatures below 325°F (160°C), do not decrease the given temperature.

| Oven description | °C | °F | Gas Mark |
|---|---|---|---|
| Cool | 110 | 225 | 1/4 |
| | 130 | 250 | 1/2 |
| Very slow | 140 | 275 | 1 |
| | 150 | 300 | 2 |
| Slow | 170 | 325 | 3 |
| Moderate | 180 | 350 | 4 |
| | 190 | 375 | 5 |
| Moderately Hot | 200 | 400 | 6 |
| Fairly Hot | 220 | 425 | 7 |
| Hot | 230 | 450 | 8 |
| Very Hot | 240 | 475 | 9 |
| Extremely Hot | 250 | 500 | 10 |

## Useful conversions

| 1/4 teaspoon | 1.25 ml |
|---|---|
| 1/2 teaspoon | 2.5 ml |
| 1 teaspoon | 5 ml |
| 1 Australian tablespoon | 20 ml (4 teaspoons) |
| 1 UK/US tablespoon | 15 ml (3 teaspoons) |

### Butter/Shortening

| 1 tablespoon | 1/2 oz | 15 g |
|---|---|---|
| 1 1/2 tablespoons | 3/4 oz | 20 g |
| 2 tablespoons | 1 oz | 30 g |
| 3 tablespoons | 1 1/2 oz | 45 g |